Everyday Struggle:

How Toxic Workspaces Impact Black Women

Presented By
Dr. Carey Yazeed

Shero Books
Subsidiary of Shero Productions, LLC
Louisiana

Shero Books, a subsidiary of Shero Productions, LLC., P.O. Box 2405, Gonzales, LA 70707

Everyday Struggle: How Toxic Workspaces Impact Black Women

For information on booking contributing-authors for signings, interviews, and speaking engagements please contact them directly via LinkedIn.

ISBN: 978-0-9850316-6-4

Printed in the United States of America

Table of Contents

"Sometimes survival is about navigating the thin line between rage and joy."

~ Malebo Sephodi

Introduction

*G*rowing up, I was constantly reminded that I had to be twice as good and work twice as hard than my white counterparts to reap the benefits many consider the American dream. Although, what my parents failed to realize is that America wasn't designed for me to reap anything but toil and labor profusely until my dying day. I drank the Kool-Aid known as the American dream, entered Corporate America, and worked tirelessly trying to rise to the top. Somewhere along the way, the masks of diversity and inclusion came off, and the whips of micro-aggressions and sexual harassment came out. I was reminded over and over again of who I really am—the most unprotected person in America, a Black woman. My parents didn't understand that no matter what they did to shield me from the lashes of abuse and oppression, I would always have to navigate racism, sexism, microaggressions, and now, as I grow older, ageism too.

To be considered a successful Black woman in America means the sistah with the melanated skin has gone through some shit.

She's ignored the underhanded "you people" remarks. She's remained silent while training her less educated and under-experienced white counterpart to become her supervisor. She's been overworked and underpaid, humiliated, and tortured. However, instead of calling it slavery or corporal punishment, Corporate America has sprayed perfume over the stench of the abuse on these white-collar plantations, where she is viewed as a modern-day slave. There have been times when she's sat in her car and cried because mentally, she was drained, but the house note was due. Sallie Mae wanted her money for the predator student loans she took out to pay for the now worthless degree that hasn't changed how white society views her—as a nigger. So she dried her eyes, fixed her lipstick while tucking in her pride, and headed back inside of the plantation that now resembles a large office building and continued to take the lashes from the whip that causes racial trauma.

As a society, we don't talk about toxic workspaces and how they impact Black women. No, we just keep our heads down and continue to be twice as good while working twice as hard. All while holding on to the belief that this country will do right by Black women one day. We know that's a lie, as being silent will only continue to hurt us.

The contributing authors of this anthology decided to disrupt the fairytale and stop sugar coating the truth of what really takes place in Corporate America. Instead of acting like "everything is okay," they dug in their stilettos to expose the racism and abuse saying, "you see, what really happened was..." Collectively, these highly educated Black women have come together to give the world a behind-the-scenes glimpse into the hell they've had to endure just to survive a nine to five and be considered a "successful Black Woman" in Corporate America by white society.

Dr. Carey Yazeed

Say My Name

Marlo R. Green, SPHR, SHRM-SCP, MOL, MBA

Abayomi Dangote looked the part in her new black pants suit with a pearl-embossed cerulean shirt, and when she stepped off the elevator, her emotions were as high as the clouds in the sky. Abayomi was elated. After years of persistence, she had completed her bachelor's degree, master's degree, two internships, and all the certifications to prove her career worthiness. She made her mother and father so proud during each stage of her success, and now, despite her apprehension, she had accepted her dream job. This was day one, and she was ready!

Abayomi attended her company's new employee orientation along with the other new hires. After the company's presenter asked her name once, then again – and again – she gave up her struggle. The presenter had given up, even before attempting to pronounce her name. Out of fear of leaving her personal comfort zone, Abayomi laid the matter to rest. "Oh, honey, we'll just have to call you Abby because your proper name is far too hard to pronounce. Abby just sounds more American. After all, you speak more like a white girl anyway. So proper!" *Abayomi gave up her struggle and smiled but said nothing.*

Orientation meetings complete. Susan, the receptionist, offered to walk Abayomi to where her new team was situated on the other side of the building. As the pair waited for the elevator, Susan exclaimed, "Abby, we are so happy to have you! I was intimidated when you first walked in the door, but then I realized you're different from the others. You're more like us than most people with foreign-sounding names, and you're so pretty for a brown girl. I wish I were tan like you!" Abayomi looked at Susan, bit her lip, and smiled.

By the time Abayomi reached her team's workspace, she was mentally exhausted and emotionally frayed. She had been looking forward to working for the company, and particularly her team's leader. Sitting down for their first one-on-one, her leader discussed the importance of diversity, equity, inclusion, and respect in the workplace. She emphasized the company values and stated how seriously they took them. All Abayomi could do was smile weakly while the events of the last couple of hours swirled in her head. A large knot began to form in her stomach.

If anyone had bothered to care, they would have discovered that Abayomi was born in America. She is—and has always been—an American citizen. Her mother so missed the happiness of her beloved Nigeria that she chose her daughter's name to forge a connection to her ancestral heritage. She often told Abayomi stories about her great-grandmother working in the Kodak Mata Dye Pit in Kano to enable a better life for her girls. Though it led Abayomi to ask herself…was this really better?

This story is not unique. Abayomi's path is sadly well worn. Many have imprinted their own footprints on it, along the way to what they hoped would be a destination of dignity, respect, and belonging. Some get there, while others do not. A gallop poll shared that more than one-fourth of the U.S. working population has experienced microaggressions in one form or another. In contrast, another rousing one-third has admitted to witnessing these microaggressions. Our institutions are still too frail to support a reasonable journey for all except for the most headstrong, the most willing to disrupt and ignore benefit-risk calculations, and those who are willing to "put it all out there." Even that is no guarantee of success or belonging.

When Serving No Longer Serves:
Social Work, Racism and a Pandemic

Cheryl Hurst, LCSW-R

"What I love about you, Cheryl, is that you speak your mind! You're always so honest and speak up in meetings. I appreciate it."

–White Female Supervisor

"You know, Cheryl, sometimes, I think…you say things that are honest, and it should be maybe more positive…"

–Same White Female Supervisor, three years later during my performance review when she denied me opportunities for a leadership promotion

"I just think, we have to be mindful about not being too negative, especially when [new staff member] is here."

–Newly Appointed White Male Supervisor during

a meeting when I confronted the program's racist policies and horrible communication.

"These parents! These parents keep having all of these children and can't manage them!"

- White Female Pediatrician, describing her perception of the Black, Latinx & immigrant families utilizing a school clinic where I worked full-time as a senior social worker.

J have countless examples of such comments made to me, a Black Social Worker serving in the healthcare field for over 17 years. I have worked tirelessly for my patients and their families. I have lent my own voice to programs within several institutions claiming to bring high-quality healthcare & advancement to underserved communities. They always market it as a way to "improve the lives of those in our care." Pausing to reflect on the mission of these institutions, juxtaposed by my experiences working with them, continues to be an illuminating parallel that remains a core issue of our nation today. Systemic. Racism.

Even in a worldwide pandemic, my voice, opinions, and ideas have been blatantly ignored. Dangerously ignored. This is all too familiar in the world of Black women. Why should working for a medical setting, supposedly aimed to serve the community of Black & Latinx families, be any different? Well, actually, it's not at all; I (re) learned this first hand.

As I reflect on the many ways my ideas & opinions have been silenced, I am stunned to be rendered silent! You see, as I worked to develop these paragraphs, the examples were many. Yet, the voice that has become nearly overpowering in my mind has been the one that repeatedly silenced me. I'm stunned to see that this minimizing, dismissing voice has now become part of my own. An internalized one that I am now forced to look at, analyze, and contextualize. It's a voice that I am currently seeking, so desperately, to ignore. It has perpetuated racism and resulted in my working within programs where I have felt unsupported, undervalued, discriminated against, invalidated, ignored, and often used. If we pretend that these circumstances don't impact service delivery, clients, and the spiritual and emotional stamina of thousands of Black women who have careers in social work, then the changes we so desperately need for our nation's reckoning with race will never truly be actualized. This chapter serves to be a pathway to my truth so that it might bring truth to other creative, intelligent, and worthy Black women in the field of social work and social services. I hope that it also serves as a call to action for medical and mental health institutions and educational institutions to take an honest look at themselves with the hope that there will be an intentional commitment to supporting, not silencing, Black women. While there are countless similar stories, this one before you is mine and mine alone.

It is incumbent on medical institutions to face their discriminatory practices, starting with their hiring practices and ending with the processes by which policies are created and instituted. While it is not a secret that so much of social work education has deep roots in white racist values, this chapter's focus is to finally speak my truth about the impact of this said education on my work in institutions that perpetuate these harmful practices. This chapter is also an invitation to the directors, supervisors, CEOs, CFOs, Presidents, and leaders of any institution that employs Black women in the field of Social Services and Higher Education. I implore you to examine your practices and curriculums to make changes, actual changes that support the talents and creativity of Black women. Diversity. Inclusion. Equity. Affinity Groups. Retaining & Recruiting staff of color. Listening Circles. A seat at the proverbial table. These are just a few of the socially trendy terms used by companies (and as hashtags) that sound conscientious and astute. Yet, ask many Black women working in any social service agency or medical institution, and they will most likely confirm that these words sound great. However, the concepts have failed to be fully and consistently implemented. Not enough attention is paid to the parallel process between service delivery and the experience of Black women working in social services. For many years, the medical institution where I worked never acknowledged my overlapping identities while working for them. Yet, in my early years working for the institution, I addressed the lack of conversations about racism, race, and ethnicity within the program and in the clinical setting (service delivery). I even presented a lecture on this very topic to the entire program and at a national conference! Years later, though, the matter has fallen to the very bottom of the list of the program's competing priorities, with the number of patients holding steady at the top.

As a Black woman who is a member of the 'underserved' Bronx community that I also served, my superiors thought nothing of silencing me or minimizing my ideas or experiences. There were whispers of this truth for many years, but the truth was shouted in my ear like Radio Raheem's boombox during the COVID-19 summer of 2020. It was expected that I adhere to being a chess piece to save face in the spirit of serving my clients. As a social worker providing therapy for Black, Caribbean & Latinx children, I am versed and connected to the children's mental health process. So when I spoke up about my own pain, anxieties, fears, and frustrations during the COVID-19 pandemic, I was thanked for my service and asked to report to potentially unsafe, dangerous settings as a dedicated employee. My director demonstrated a refusal to listen to my concerns or honor my fears and requests to provide the same quality of my services while working from home.

I clearly saw that her vision was not for our patients or my health and safety. It was actually to demonstrate that she could direct her staff to where they were called to be to show her power, maintain her status, and paternalistic management style. One week before this health crisis was coined "The Pandemic," I remember sitting at a computer at my program's administrative office. Rumors abound with the seriousness of what was to come but the energy, while uncertain, was primarily void of clear communication from my 'leadership team.' While there was much to be discovered, the stance seemed to be, "don't ask, don't tell, wait until we tell you." Several hours into my workday, I was approached by a director who released me to return home, saying my role (as a social worker) was 'non-essential' and that I would be contacted for any next steps on where and how I was to report to work. To clarify, I worked in a Bronx public school (otherwise known as a satellite site of the main hospital campus). Since the NYC Dept of Education was scrambling to figure out how on earth to educate children during a stunning horror movie, it was understandable that I was deemed non-essential. In fact, other times when NYC schools were closed (during a snow blizzard, for example), several staff members in our program were informed that non-essential staff could take the option to use a personal or vacation day. I was always told I was a non-essential staff member, meaning I was not the one to be called during a medical emergency. While this phrase became loaded when the worldwide pandemic began, I have actually been told this on multiple occasions in the past as a hospital employee. Non-essential staff were usually the non-medical providers who did not work at the main campus. So, it made sense that I would not be 'needed' in the urgent capacity in the way a Medical Doctor, Nurse Practitioner, Registered Nurse, or Licensed Practicing Nurse might be needed to administer medical care in a crisis. I made my way home. Like many, this moment is one frozen in my memory while the world turned on its axis, rendering so much of what we understood to be our normal ways of interacting and living.

I remember talking to my colleagues not too soon after that, as many of us wondered what was to come. The schools where we worked daily shut their doors while the hospitals were busting theirs open with this looming, terrifying virus. I attended countless educational lectures on SARS-CoV-2, COVID19 that advised me to wash my hands more frequently and for longer than usual. I was taught the symptoms should one of my child or adolescent patients have any and advised to send them to the pediatrician I worked with for a medical assessment. As the information poured in, so did the panic. The program I worked for scrambled to make sense of the emerging realities, they were faced with needing to transform the work for hundreds of staff. While they scrambled, they seldom communicated effectively, thoroughly, or at all. My director began to assign her staff to work in areas of the hospital, often sending an email three minutes before the end of our shift. This stunned all of us. The expectations were unclear at best and when I sought clarification as to what my role or tasks would be working in a completely different arena than I've worked for years, I was thanked for my dedication and service. I was told to report to an emergency room and that additional information would be provided to me when I arrived. Was I to provide care, enter demographic information, interview prospective and incoming patients? Who would provide care for my patients during my "deployment?" How long would this assignment be? Instead of getting answers to these questions, I was acknowledged for my "service." This mandate demonstrated apparent negligence for my patients and a total lack of regard for my own safety. There is much focus on the finances needed to keep the doors open for anyone not familiar with social service agencies or hospitals. Translation: it's often a numbers game. A sad reality means I am to generate a certain number of visits per day. This focus on numbers (quantity) over quality speaks to a particular set of white racist values. Likewise, when I made attempts to express my discomfort about working in an emergency room without proper protective personal equipment (PPE) or a clear assignment of tasks, this is when I learned that as a union member, to grieve an assignment, I had to first show up. I felt like my hands were tied, and my voice was dismissed.

I started to question our union's effectiveness and support in real-time when I noticed that several of my newly hired mental health colleagues were not being "deployed" to multiple sites as frequently as I was. I was a senior social worker, and unfortunately, I wrongfully believed I would have seniority over others in times like this. I believed that my title would account for something other than a title. While this might be accurate on paper, when leadership teams lack diverse opinions and lead with "their way is the only way to lead," no other voices are considered. Shockingly, after that day in which I was assigned to work in an emergency room, I would like to say the leadership of my division came to their senses. Despite having no experience in this setting, which was also ignored when I pointed this out. They heard my pleas and allowed me to conduct my work by providing therapy to children and teenagers from home. This is logical. I could ensure my own safety and continue to do the work I enjoy doing. Yet, no, that wasn't the case. In the first three months of the COVID-19 pandemic (March 2020—June 2020), I was assigned to multiple locations, further exposing me to the virus and certainly putting my life, as well as my loved ones, at risk. When all of NYC shut down, I was suddenly told I was "essential." Even the subway system shut down, which was a true sign of our now dire stunning reality. What a mixed message this was! While I have always known my work to be essential, suddenly I was told that my role in a setting that seldom acknowledged my worth was essential but that my life wasn't to be protected. At the time, I wasn't able to process the trauma of these messages. Yet, it was familiar. When my requests were denied, it was the same overtone–just do what is expected of you, Cheryl, you don't speak up or ask questions. You just do as you're told because you are a body. This notion is deeply ingrained in the Social Work profession: Social Workers are unsung heroes who serve others but never themselves. A Social Worker's career is that of a selfless individual who gives solely in service to others. I have experienced the damaging impact of these messages in real-time in the health care and social service agencies where I have worked.

I remember confessing to a colleague the terror I felt about losing my life to this horrible virus as so many of my Black community members have due to the racist medical system I had dedicated thousands of hours of my life to. I vividly remember riding a NYC bus early one weekday morning on my way to work, yet to another ambulatory clinic. When I boarded the bus searching for a seat, I noticed that every passenger was a woman of color. I saw the terror

I was feeling in their eyes peering back at me as I looked at the other passengers. My white supervisor and probably their white supervisors who dictated their agendas were careless, disinterested, and cold. During my "deployment," the supervisors created agendas and spreadsheets wherein my colleagues were asked to work on parent presentations on how to help their children thrive during online learning. These supervisors failed to realize that so many families didn't have consistent wifi connections or even sufficient devices to facilitate online learning! One of our directors sent an email asking us to take photos of ourselves reaching out to our patients for a PR ad showing the hospital workers demonstrated commitment to our patients. I was appalled. All the while, I continued to advocate for myself to work from home while my family and friends watched and prayed in horror. Again, my request was met with a superficial acknowledgment of my work ethic and dedication but ultimately fell on deaf ears. I was repeatedly reminded that I was essential, and since there wasn't any current work-from-home policy, it wasn't possible. It seems that if there were ANY time to create a new policy, such as one allowing staff to work from home, a worldwide pandemic would be it! It was an infuriating and terrifying experience. While I watched my community die before my eyes, another brutal act of racist violence played out in front of me.

This is perhaps the most profound and painful reality of this experience. When Derek Chauvin murdered George Floyd and when police officers murdered Breonna Taylor while she lay in her bed, I was stunned by my program's failure to acknowledge these devastating murders, all the while putting me in harms' way. I and a very small group of my colleagues, spoke out against these injustices and confronted my bosses for their stunning silence. More than five days later, it was met with more silence followed by a reluctant acknowledgment for their desire for everyone to come together. Their silence was yet another example of my personal work experiences. The signs were clear—I, my feelings, and my safety were of little importance. My boss informed me that the hospital wasn't a social justice institution and that they couldn't make any statements that might be perceived in the wrong way. I was stunned silent, this time by their callousness. Since Mr. Floyd's death, there have been at least 229 murders of Black people at the hands of police, as confirmed by Newsweek. There have been over 600,000 deaths from COVID-19 and complications therein. At least 15% have been Black patients. While I have been blessed to live long enough to tell this story—my story—I continue to reclaim my voice and the truth of my experience.

The reality is this: often, when Black women confront systems oppression (in the workplace or otherwise), occasionally we are thanked for being honest or vocal. However, more often, we are pacified with superficial compliments about how hard we work or how dedicated we are. Yet, these so-called compliments never translated to my promotion and only served to maintain the status quo of an all-white leadership to keep me silent. My opinion and my truth have been dismissed, minimized, or centered by someone else. The many many times I've confronted poor practices laden in bias, either at a macro (program-wide, agency level) or micro-level (interpersonal microaggressions), I was described with the age of tropes reserved for Black women—"angry" or "too sensitive." This is yet another white racist value in which speaking up to those in power is met with defensiveness which perpetuates an oppressive work environment. Equating the raising of problematic issues with being "angry" demonstrates what happens when those in power are fearful of addressing difficult topics that may challenge their perceived place of power, which they desperately cling to.

It's ironic to facilitate healing pediatric patients while working for programs that have been anything but healing. They have caused irreparable emotional and physical harm. I have finally realized that my service no longer serves me—my well-being or my spirit. The devastating reality is how many Black women get used to and become numb to this work experience. The apathy and defeat are real. The student loan debt, mortgages, and financial responsibilities create a vicious cycle of practical reasons, so many Black women remain in painful work environments. While some of you are reading this chapter, you may feel your bias rearing its head with a comment like, 'Oh, but that's not every work environment. I'm sure she just worked in one that was old, out of touch, and poorly run. No place is perfect, and she should be lucky she had a stable job when much-experienced unemployment and financial hardships.' While, yes, these statements might be accurate descriptions of the program where I worked but employment at what cost? Remaining in a toxic, unsupportive work environment has lasting effects. I now honestly acknowledge that I am facing the heartbreaking truth that all Black people continue to be slapped with time and time again. Systems such as large corporations, businesses, and even those in the field of healthcare, wellness, and mental health, take a very long time to change, if at all. The ingredients to make and sustain changes that address systemic racism are not reliant on the Black community or other communities of color. The truth is, I am tired. The truth is that many Black people are drained but still continue to show up at places of employment that perpetuate elitist attitudes and supremacist culture values.

I know my experience is not unique regarding the chronicity of Black women's voices, ideas, expertise, and creativity being ignored, minimized, silenced, dismissed, or even stolen in the workplace. Though, here are suggestions on what can be done to start the healing process. This is my call to action.

For Undergraduate and Graduate Schools of Social Work Practice (and all mental health professions): Accept students that might not always fit the 'mold' of highest test scores, parental income, or grade point average. It's well known that many students cannot always afford prep courses or tutoring. Instead, ensure expanded searches for incoming candidates who demonstrate a vested interest, creativity, drive, and willingness to bring new and fresh ideas to their school community. Listen to those students and provide a space for their voices to be heard. Develop curriculum committees staffed with individuals with varied life experiences and listen to them.

Include diverse authors throughout the reading list/curriculums! Recently, I attended a postgraduate psychoanalytic continuing education class in which there wasn't a single POC clinician on the course reading list! Continuously revisit and revise the curriculums to ensure inclusivity for student learning. Provide students who express interest in any given area of clinical practice, policy, group work, hospice, or medical care, an opportunity to work with a mentor to further develop their skills in preparation for their professional career development.

For Faculty: Mandate ongoing professional development for all teaching and administrative staff members interacting with students. Hire Black professors! While this seems simple enough, as an adjunct lecturer at two New York City universities, my students have expressed surprise when they meet me, professing they haven't had a Black professor before. Shockingly disappointing, I know. Offer leadership positions to non-white staff members such as search committees, research committees, and committees to develop curriculums (see above). The absence of Black women on such committees perpetuates the myth that Black women are not qualified to give their perspectives or expertise. Provide Black lecturers and professionals opportunities to present their work in many different arenas, such as campus-wide, nationally, or internationally. Uplift the hard work and dedication of Black women in your setting. Not with superficial compliments but with opportunities for professional growth to retain their creativity and intelligence.

For Medical and Social Service Institutions: All medical licensing boards should require all professionals to attend anti-racist courses to renew their annual licensure.

Give credit where it's due, not just for credit's sake. Listen to Black women's ideas on creating new policies—even if those policies haven't existed before! That's what's new. For agencies to truly call themselves service agencies, wellness, or healthcare institutions, they cannot expect to expand their reach by doing the same old things.

Consider the pathway to policy creation: were there only two people from similar life experiences creating these policies, or were there various voices? Do those in leadership only create procedures, or do they also include perspectives from those on the ground? Have these policies included a range in attitudes before actually being instituted? Is the care being provided anti-discriminatory? How do you know? What systems have been put in place to revisit the anti-discrimination practices continuously?

Offer ongoing, consistent, supportive opportunities to ensure Black women's success in your institutions. This includes but is certainly not limited to equal pay. How have those who have perpetrated microaggressions towards patients, clients, and even staff been held accountable? During my tenure, I was told the only way microaggressions could be addressed was if I wrote a document detailing the incidents. This expectation is another form of controlling communication style—the belief that if it's not written down, it holds no relevance or didn't happen. While my first language is English, and I possess the privilege of many years of education, I can adequately express myself through writing and verbal communication; however, this one way of communicating and documenting hinders many groups of people. Placing value on this way of communicating silences the experiences of those who may not feel comfortable with the written word. Institutions should seek other opportunities to communicate to ensure all staff can express their truth in a way that's comfortable for them.

Finally, to retain Black and POC people as staff, leaders of academic and wellness (including medical and mental health) institutions must validate, believe, and act on ending Black people's experiences of racism in the workplace. Yes, sometimes this means looking at existing policies, creating new ones, revising curriculums to be more inclusive of various lived experiences, examining hiring practices, closing the pay gap but most importantly, pledging to hold up the mirror and look inward for the change. Without this commitment to engage in difficult conversations, ongoing learning, and change, the cycle of harm will continue to deter the crucial healing that needs to be done. As for me, I'm sure you've already guessed the ending of my story. Yes, I resigned and this chapter sharing my truth is my new beginning.

3

Just Another Day

Dr. Tracy Daniel-Hardy

"*What shit am I going to have to deal with today?*" That is the question that often comes to mind on mornings like this immediately after checking my phone to see how much time I have left to snooze. I usually shuffle a bit in the bed after nudging my husband to get up. Then, I breathe deeply and thank God for allowing me to see another day. I then exhale slowly and let one foot hit the floor before sliding the other one down. As I think about what I want to wear, I take my medicine and walk to the closet room to turn on the iron. I ask the good Lord to give me strength, guide my tongue, and help me not to wear my emotions on my face so Danielle, my friend and colleague, won't have to text me to fix my face during whatever meeting I have to sit through today.

As I am ironing, I try to anticipate anything that might happen in the meeting today. What is on the agenda that might get me pulled into a discussion? How many meetings before the meeting occurred? (Breathe slowly and methodically, Tracy!) Did my secretary get everything on the board agenda? Now I start my mad dash to finish getting ready for the day. I unplug the iron, transport my freshly ironed clothes to the bedroom, turn on the curling irons, check my blood pressure, do my squats, get in the shower, and start the thinking process again. What are they up to? "Ah....that's it. That's it," I think to myself. That's what they are trying to do. Everything becomes so clear while in the shower. I finish and get dressed to start my day.

I guess you can say that I am tired before I even get to work because I am tired of them talking to me like I am crazy. I am tired of them ignoring the policies and procedures because they do not want to acknowledge me in my role. I am so tired of them running to tell "Big Daddy" (Mr. Dickens) on me while crying those precious and fake tears. The same kind that got Emmitt Till killed. Only because I did not give them what they wanted or I did something they disapproved of. Although he knows they are full of shit, he calls me anyway to follow up behind those tears. It used to catch me off-guard, but now I can predict how long it will take him to call me in.

The tears on this particular day started after a conversation with another colleague. Let's call her Becky. Becky called. It must be noted here that Becky tries hard to avoid having to call me at all. However, she did on this day in particular because others could not access the files that she'd shared. The program that Becky used was one that we'd blocked years prior because it allowed students to circumvent our web filter. Becky had spent several hours working on the files at home and was ready to publish them but found them blocked. I explained to her what the problem was and why. I almost felt bad that she'd spent so much time creating the files that probably could not be used. I only almost felt bad for her because there was another approved and widely used program that we'd been using for many years that she decided not to use. I told her that I'd see what we could do to prevent the students from using the program to circumvent the filter.

After finishing the phone call with her, I spoke with my network engineer about making an exception. Together, he and I decided to make the exception to ensure the students were still blocked from using the program. I called her back to inform her of the good news, but she didn't answer. I knew. I just knew she'd run down to the other end of their building to "tell on me" to Mr. Dickens. Within minutes, my phone rang. When I noticed Mr. Dickens' number on the Caller ID, I shook my head because I KNEW what the call was regarding. In a very overly calm way, he told me that Becky had come to his office upset and crying about all of the work she'd done that was being blocked by our web filter. I continued to shake my head in disbelief that she'd immediately ran down to his office to tell on me again. Evidently, he felt sorry for her and was compelled to rescue her from big, bad me. I was trying to control my breathing while he told me about Becky's tears. I explained that we had already taken care of her issue and informed him why we had the program blocked. I thought he would be more concerned about protecting our data and the network. Instead, he was more concerned about Becky's tears. I hung up the phone, screamed out loudly, shook my head in disbelief, and slammed my hands on the desk. I felt like I was competing with a spoiled and cocky teenager whose father believed his daughter was the perfect child. Due to Becky and her crew, these types of conflicts have seen an increase. Oh, how I longed for the days before all of the office politics and tantrums.

Life was so much simpler when I was in that high school classroom at the end of the hall on the second floor near the elevator. One had to want to see me to come up the stairs and walk down the hall to my classroom. It was dark and even a bit scary in the mornings when no one else was in the hallway. As I look back, I think about how peaceful and simple it was back then. I was innocent (or naïve) and probably missed many microaggressions. As I recollect, I believed that since I was credentialed and knew my craft, I was less likely to be on the receiving end of racism, prejudice, or bias. I knew I wasn't exempt, but I thought I was safer within my profession because I'd worked so hard to earn the right to be there. Of course, I was wrong. In some ways, that made it worse for me.

I probably heard or felt some of the microaggressions, but I did not know how to process them or what to do with them when I did identify them. I often wonder if I am a bit sensitive right now instead of how I was back then. Am I too alert? Is it the current political and social climate making me hyper-aware, or has it become more profound as I've moved up to the leadership table? Hmm! I predict it's a mix of all of these elements.

I think I missed a significant amount of microaggressions when I was in that little classroom upstairs at the end of the hallway. I thought that I worked with good-hearted people who cared about students meaning they had to care about me, or so I thought. They had to care about all students because they taught all students. As I look back, I realize there were, indeed, many good-hearted teachers and administrators who truly loved and cared for the students. Even Mrs. Hancock seemed to care about all children. She always made a point to tell me how appalled she was because I'd parked in her unofficial but known parking spot. Then there was Mr. Simmons. We didn't talk much even though we were right across the hall from each other. When he spoke to me, he was cordial and may have even smiled every now and then.

However, when he dealt with Black or Brown boys, he was as mean as a snake. He took every opportunity to correct them loudly and submit a disciplinary form on them. He would verbally jump them in such a disrespectful and demeaning way that they would bounce back at him in an equally disrespectful manner. That seemed to satisfy him because he'd quickly whip out the pen to write them up. After witnessing it a few times and noticing that it only happened with Black and Brown boys, I began to intervene. I would get the young men's attention by calling their names or walking over to them to pat them on the shoulder or back gently. I would look them directly in the eyes, shake my head to indicate my disapproval, and tell them to keep their mouths shut. I'd inform them that lashing out to him would make it worse and that there was no way this would benefit them. Doing this did not disrespect Mr. Simmons, but it let him know that I saw him for who he really was. It also protected the young men from disciplinary action if they listened to me.

I find it interesting that just as I protected those young Black and Brown boys from Mr. Simmons, I have to think daily about how to protect myself from being mistreated or ignored while trying not to be 'the angry, Black woman.' It's overwhelming, but now it's the end of the day. I'm exhausted. I still have work to do before I shut it down for the day. I'm worn out on days like this because I have spent so much time bobbing and weaving like a champion boxer in the ring with a formidable opponent through the microaggressions, the calls regarding the fake tears, and embellished stories. All of this taking my focus instead of working on other things that require my attention. It's now 4:00 pm, and some of my staff are easing their doors closed and tipping out before they have to participate in my "second wind" of work.

I yell goodbye to them to acknowledge that I see them tipping out, make notes of what I wanted to discuss with them, and sigh as I begin to complete some work that has been waiting on me all day. I check my phone messages and my mailbox that sits on the wall in my secretary's office. I check in with her now that it's quiet in our hall. I take one final look at my email and decide which email requires an immediate response and which can wait until later before logging out. I look at the phone in anticipation of one final call from Mr. Dickens before I leave for the day. I walk slowly to the door and turn off the light. I take one last look back at my desk. My direct line doesn't ring again, so I close the door and give a deep sigh of relief because I made it through another day!

The walk down the hall and out the door to the elevator is one of mixed emotions. I am happy to be leaving this place on this day, but I am also a bit somber as I know I will repeat this struggle tomorrow morning. I must mention that not every day is like this, but too many days are. I should also mention that it has not always been an everyday struggle. A regime change in an integral department brought an element of toxicity with it. I was not interrogated or antagonized as long as I complied with their requests and didn't ask questions.

After making it off the elevator and out the door, I stop for one final conversation with Mo, my custodian, as I listen to her on my way to the car and offer the response she dreads but expects from me. I am reminded of some things that help me even today to endure the everyday struggle:

- Make it a practice to always do what's right no matter who is doing wrong and getting away with it. People of color are usually not extended the same grace as others, whether the failure to follow the rules is intentional or not.
- Know the policies and procedures for yourself and know what is commonly practiced.
- Don't assume the other persons of color in your organization will be your allies, even if their experience is similar to yours.
- Make time to document interactions with dates, times, people, location, and descriptions of the interaction.
- Try to maintain your composure, but understand that it is part of human nature to have emotions.
- Find healthy outlets that allow you to decompress and recharge.
- Take special care of your physical and mental health.
- Don't work yourself to death to make an impression. When you are gone, your position will probably be posted or filled sooner than you think it would.
- Find one or a few work allies who can encourage, challenge you and tap you on the shoulder when necessary.
- Have an exit plan ready to execute when it's time to go. Consider a side hustle that could become your main hustle when it's time to resign.

After I end my conversation with Mo, I crank up my car and the music; I slowly pull out of the parking garage and away from the struggle for today.

Social Work Blues

Mylonne Sullivan, MSW, LSW, LICDC

*I*nclusivity has been a term used frequently but often does not extend to Black women as regularly as it should. Historically, Black people have been passed up for employment opportunities, denied access to housing funds, received poor medical attention, limited educational resources, and incarcerated at excessively high rates. Black Women, experiencing a double portion of oppression, continue to have difficulty being included in leadership. Even when chosen, they may experience difficulty with being allowed to make decisions, particularly within a patriarchal and capitalist society.

We live in a society where many of the same cultural norms created by this country remain. Of course, these norms do not look the exact same, but women have been historically excluded from all major 'systems' in the USA. It is challenging to live in a country that prides itself on assimilation, does not give room for differences, or even celebrates uniqueness. I have spoken to so many Black Women who desire to belong, be accepted, and be heard in various spaces, including myself. I have worked extremely hard to be seen and heard as a Black woman millennial. Often, especially due to being the youngest Black woman in most meetings I attend or in leadership, I put a lot of effort into being seen and heard.

I remember in my childhood being told consistently that I had to work twice as hard and be twice as good. I was often given the advice that when I entered the workforce, to be sure to come in to work early and to ensure I stayed late to be given an opportunity of advancement. I was told I would not be seen as a person who should get job opportunities for meeting minimum qualifications. Nor would I have the ability to be recognized for average work ethics. I remember being told that I needed to consistently work harder than my white counterparts; so that doors that would typically be close to me would be a jar. My parents and relatives explained that their advice was the minimum expectation, but it did not mean opportunities would not be given to me because I came to work two hours early or 60 hours a week. My efforts would only crack the door for the opportunity to be presented. These speeches highlighted that I could still not walk through doors of opportunity or be included in decision-making conversations even when I accepted leadership positions. They further explained that I might encounter harsh words or treatment in the workplace.

As I got older, eventually, the conversation shifted to explain that I would never be respected in the way I believed I should. They further explained that I may encounter harsh words or treatment in the workplace. So, I'd better be the best, so I can demand the best. I had to ensure that I was the best to be invited to important discussions and other closed-door conversations. To be sure, I set my own rules for salary and the cost of my services because I will be consistently 'lowballed' due to being a Black woman. When negotiating salary, I always ask for more money because the worst someone can tell me is 'no.'

I was told the game of life was set up to be grateful for opportunities and say yes because I am a Black woman. I should just be excited about the opportunity presented, not that I have skills, knowledge, or experience. I should hail with excitement for any chance, not because I was qualified for any particular position, but being a Black woman provided me with some options.

These messages rang so clear, and they followed me throughout adulthood and shaped how I saw myself in the world, so much that with any opportunity presented, I had to work hard. I had to network and create opportunities for myself. The opportunities would have never come because we live in a society where Black women are often rendered for their expertise but are not provided the same compensation as their white counterparts.

I remember being in undergrad and working four jobs simultaneously, being involved in three to five leadership positions at any given time, trying to network, and considering long-term goal planning. I had to learn to manage the messages I received growing up because they began to create a consistent cycle of being overworked, although compensated, but overworked nonetheless. I have had numerous opportunities, and I took advantage of all of them. I consistently reflect on how those experiences have impacted how I engage in my current workspace, including the rigid boundaries with coworkers, making the daily choice to take up space, and advocate for myself and others within conflict. As much as I was trained and 'prepared' for these experiences, each time I was still caught off guard and experienced some form of racism, it still shook me to my core.

I remember working for a nonprofit agency located in one of the most historically racist cities near Cleveland, OH. The police frequently targeted black staff who worked in this city. We were never given citations but frequently pulled over for one reason or another. In addition to being targeted by the police in this city, we were also gaslighted by the administration in various scenarios related to inequity and microaggressions in the workplace.

Merriam Webster defines microaggressions as "a comment or action that subtly and often unconsciously or unintentionally expresses a prejudiced attitude toward a member of a marginalized group (such as a racial minority)." The most important factor regarding a microaggression is that the intent of the person expressing attitude or comment is less important than the impact of the person experiencing the microaggression. In other words, no one cares if they didn't intend to offend, they did.

A perfect example of a microaggression I experienced was with a coworker over my hair. Being a black woman in the workplace, I've often told my family members that my natural hair would never be accepted. I've been told to wear my hair straight or in very "neat" styles because it is unprofessional. I distinctly remember a scenario where I was sitting at a desk awaiting a client to arrive for a scheduled session. I remember feeling a hand in my hair. At the time, I wore an afro. One of my co-workers placed their hand in my afro, their fingers grazing my scalp. Mortified would not accurately describe how I felt. Violated would be a more accurate description. In addition to feeling enraged, my coworker decided to invade my space and touch me without permission. I was a person who had autonomy over my own body and that my hair was attached to the body that I owned.

I wondered what made her believe that she could touch me. PRIVILEGE. I had to address her and inform her of the inappropriateness, especially the unprofessionalism, including describing how uncomfortable the experience was for me. I believe my face told her of the message before I could articulate my words. She instantly responded, "I am so sorry, I didn't think that you would mind. I just love your hair, and I just want to feel it because it's different". I took moments to respond, which felt like minutes, to gather what I would say. I had to consider how I would relay the inappropriate nature of her behavior to her, so I did. The organization already experienced white staff feeling 'attacked' or believing Black staff should see their intentions, not their actions. Many of the Black female staff, including myself, were aware of the 'angry Black woman' stereotype and did not want the perception within the workplace.

Another microaggression I experienced involved a different coworker and my name. I remember my parents telling me how my name was chosen. There wasn't a special meaning. They just liked the way it sounded. My father was intentional about choosing a name that would disguise my ethical background or even the gender I possessed. As I entered the workplace, I've had so many experiences of feeling uncomfortable with co-workers and supervisors mispronouncing my name and being unwilling to work towards pronouncing it correctly. As I grew older and my advocacy for others increased, my willingness to challenge others equally increased. More specifically, I was working at a nonprofit agency, and a white male coworker walked up to me, saying, "Hi Malone (correct pronunciation is My-Lohn), how are you"? As I replied with the correct pronunciation and answer to his question, he gave me a look to say, 'How dare you correct me? I was just checking on you.' The unfortunate part of this experience was that he did not apologize for the mispronunciation nor attempted to correct himself. Instead, he chuckled and stated, "Calm down, I was just kidding. I know that's how you pronounce your name," but he proceeded to mispronounce it yet again.

The two examples above may seem minor, but if they are frequent, the frustration of always speaking up can be overwhelming and often exhausting. Being a licensed social worker and chemical dependency counselor in management, I have encountered many types of people. I have consistently spoken up for myself but have also had times where I did not address racially influenced behaviors. Although there may be moments where I do not put forth effort for myself, I always pride myself on advocating for my clients.

To provide more context, in 2016, I was a Case Manager, still in school for my Master's of Social Work. I sat in a hospital emergency room with a Black male client who needed to be admitted to a psychiatric hospital. The hospital refused to admit this client because the client was high risk and had been admitted "too many times." As I advocated for this Black client to receive services with a nurse and doctor in a space that often doesn't listen to Black women, I felt angered, small, unheard, and disregarded. However, I continued advocating for my client, as often, Black women have to do for our community and families.

Some people may attribute the condescending tone and the unsympathetic facial expressions that I witnessed to these medical staff members acting as part of the medical model. Contrary to popular belief, despite being in a helping profession, I have experienced similar attitudes, facial expressions, and unwelcoming body language towards clients repeatedly by white counterparts across various fields. Particularly, instances of those in positions of power. The exertion of that power leading others to follow so blindly and quickly is exacerbating. In scenarios like this, where someone is powerless and unable to make their own decisions, let alone at times, tying their own shoes is hurtful to witness.

Although I continued to speak with the medical staff to get my client admitted into this hospital, I felt small and angered. I'm advocating for myself and someone else who cannot advocate on their own. The nurse and doctor I spoke with overused words like "people like him… they can't keep entering our doors…." As I responded and analyzed their words, I couldn't help but wonder how my client felt. They spoke about him as if he was not in the room. As if he could not hear us or as if he was unable to speak.

Working with this particular Black man and so many like him, I sensed his fear. I feel that he was in a place familiar to him due to previous psychiatric admittance but still had a sense of fear that flashed over his face. This fear was evident in the trembles of his handles and his voice lowering as he spoke. His fear was attributed to his own hallucinations or delusions, yet the interactions with the medical staff intensified these symptoms. Bottom line, the fear was still present; whether you had a psychotherapy background or not, it was evident. Unfortunately, it seemed as if the medical staff only saw him as a threat.

Black men are consistently seen as threats, even when their own fear is present. His very presence intimidated them even when there were no signs of threats or evidence of danger. I believe they were fearful of his height and weight, but I wholeheartedly believe he was more scared than they were. I believed they did not want him in their hospital anymore because of what they perceived about the potential harm he caused the staff or the potential cost he could make by damaging the equipment within the hospital. He did not have violent behaviors, but there are many instances where people experiencing psychosis can become violent.

After spending time explaining the potential backlash via consequences of this client committing suicide after leaving the hospital premises, a possible lawsuit by the client's family, and the threat of contact from administrators at my agency; the client was finally admitted.

While at the hospital, my client did not speak the entire time when the medical staff asked him a question. First, he paused and then looked to me for validation to respond. It was as if he was a small child wanting affirmation from a parent to feel safe, and each time I permitted him to speak freely as he wanted to or not. As he continued to look my way, I nodded my head, verbalizing an 'okay' and at times saying, "Keep going. It's OK to give them more information if you want." I saw the amount of trust he gave me in those moments and in different experiences in the past with medical staff. He and other clients needed to continue to feel safe in my presence as I adhered to the social work ethics by advocating for this client and ensuring his safety needs were met physically, emotionally, mentally, and morally.

During that same week, I needed to process. I needed to discuss the frustrations of not being heard and our agency client being dismissed at the hospital. I wanted to recall the looks of the nurses when they saw my client with my supervisor, with whom I have had positive experiences with. I needed him to understand that those nurses gave looks that sent a message of disapproval and fear of this 200+ pound 6-foot Black man who was clearly in a state of psychosis.

Let's fast forward to the discussion I had with my supervisor, *"Hey, can we talk for a minute? I need to process this experience I had this week with a hospital."* I gave the demographics of the client and detailed the experience. My supervisor's response was, *"Well, does it have to be because he was Black, was he just scary because you know how clients can be."* At that moment, I stopped. I didn't have the energy to explain his words, mirrored microaggressions or the historical context of Black people in the medical field, or my current need for comfort, processing, and space without feedback.

Now, I was stuck. I needed to process this response, plus my interaction with the hospital staff. I felt exhausted. I left the office in search of some type of validation that what I experienced was true. I needed confirmation that what I felt like I was encountering was a form of gaslighting.

Merriam-Webster dictionary defines gaslighting as, "to attempt to make (someone) believe that he or she [or they] is going insane." When experiencing gaslighting, it involves the truth being distorted. It can be intentional or unintentional. Also, gaslighting is rooted in manipulation and attempts to make someone believe that they are not accurate. I believe it was unintentional, but it did not help. In his privilege, my supervisor could not understand my experience, so I removed myself from further mental fatigue to preserve the energy that I had left with him that day.

Thankfully though, I had four amazing Black women who were working with me at this time that provided a level of support that I didn't even know that I needed. After talking with them about the scenario at the hospital and my engagement with my supervisor, I felt heard. One of my coworkers, now a friend, stated, *"Damn girl, I'm sorry that happened."* Those words were the first thing that came out of her mouth after I described my day. There was a literal sense of relief throughout my body. Someone else who understood the complexities of being Black in various systems validated my experience. This is not to suggest that validation each time I experienced racism is wanted, but I longed for it in this scenario.

If I can offer any advice to you reading this: **SPEAK.** Even if your voice trembles with fear. Remember you belong in that room and at that table. To quote John Lewis, "Get in good trouble, necessary trouble, and help redeem the soul of America." **BE BOLD**. However, be sure to maintain your integrity. Remember that this society was not made for you to prosper, so follow the advice of Kenneth Hagin to 'create the world you want to see.' Just be sure to allow no one to talk you out of it, not even yourself. Remember to rest. The world will place enough stress on you, learn to take that vacation regularly, spend time with loved ones, eat well, and get the number of hours of sleep you need at night. Be sure to find a community, whether at work or outside of work, to help.

5

Dare To Dream

Dawn D. Robinson, EE, JD, PMP, SSGB

*I*n the Beginning

The 2020 movie "One Night in Miami," directed by Regina King, depicted my time growing up. Martin Luther King, Malcolm X, Jim Brown, Sam Cooke, and Cassius Clay, who changed his name to Muhammad Ali. We had the Queen of Soul, Aretha Franklin, Harry Belafonte, James Brown, Dick Gregory, and many more. They were our leaders, our voice, our inspiration. It gave us a sense of pride to have these prominent Black figures in our life, watching some of them on the "Ed Sullivan/Johnny Carson's Shows." There was Bill Cosby, on "Eye Spy," Diahann Carrol, the first Black woman to star in a non-servant role on "Julia," the Flip Wilson Show- Geraldine and Sidney Poitier, a Black doctor engaged to a white woman in "Guess Who's Coming to Dinner?"

Our rich African American History was muzzled and

eliminated from the history books. We were not taught that our great Black slave ancestors were brilliant masonries and architects who built Washington DC's capital and white house. The Tuskegee Airmen, Union Black soldiers in the Civil war, and so on. We did not learn anything about ourselves except for the fact that it was George Washington Carver who discovered the "Peanut" and, of course, George Washington, "I cannot tell a lie." Oh! How Columbus "Discovered America" when there were already indigenous African people here before he landed.

Times were hard, from the economic struggles of our people, and once Malcolm X was assassinated and then Martin Luther King, we were pushed to the brink. As a child growing up in East Baltimore, Maryland (Be-More), I remember looking out of the window of 1035 Orleans Street Apt 6J watching people running with clothes, TVs, and fires burning. There were armored tanks, with guys at the top armed with guns rolling down that same street that I crossed every day to go to Belair Market or shop on Gay Street or walk to St. James and St. John's Catholic school, which was where I got my formal education. Across the nation, cities were on fire, known now as the "60s riots."

People were angry, disenfranchised, and distraught due to the systemic racism plaguing our cities since the great Black migration North from the South. The assassinations were designed to kill our spirit. It was as though all hope was gone. Every time we had a Black leader that was for the people, they were ultimately killed. Being a resilient people, the Black Power movement was born and had evolved. In 1968 at the Olympics in Mexico City, Tommie Smith and John Carlos raised their Black fists to the sky as the crowd booed while the National Anthem was played. We still celebrate and use that iconic symbol today!

This was also our time where we had Black socially conscious music: Temptations', A Ball of Confusion, *"People moving out, People moving in-whyyy? Because of the color of their skin... Run...Run...Run, but you sure can't hide- Rap On—Brother...Rap— On...Segregation—Determination—Demonstration—Integration—*

Aggravation–Humiliation–Obligation to our Nation–Ball of Confusion"; What's Going On? by Marvin Gaye *"Mother, Mother there's too many of you crying. Brother Brother Brother, there's far too many of you dying ...you know we got to find a way- to bring some loving here today...Picket Lines -Sista and Picket Signs — Sista. Don't punish me — Sista with Brutality;"* and, Gil Scott Heron, THE REVOLUTION WILL NOT BE Televised. *"You will not be able to stay home, brother. You will not be able to plug in, turn on and cop out....You will not be able to lose yourself on skag...The Revolution will not be televised... The Revolution will not be televised."*

Unfortunately, at a very tender age, I experienced racism. Not racism between Black and whites, but racism amongst ourselves-Blacks. At the age of seven, as a 2nd grader, I quickly learned that the lighter you were with long "good hair," you were treated differently. Good hair where girls only had to apply water and Ultra Sheen hair grease to make their hair straight like our counterpart white girls. They did not need a straightening comb or had to put a towel around their necks to avoid being burned from the hot-pressing grease. That is just the way it was and maybe still is today, but the truth of the matter was we were doing it to ourselves.

I grew up in majority Black, sometimes mixed neighborhoods of various classes and sizes. When I attended Western High School, the premier school for girls in Baltimore city, it was there that another reality set in—the "class" structure. Girls from across the city came from parents who were doctors, lawyers, dentists, psychiatrists, judges, ministers, principals, teachers, and some who had no social-economic background, except hard-working blue-collar families. At that time, it was a well-integrated school, so I had white and Black friends. It was cool because this was during the 70s and Black awareness was abundant. After all, we were the generation growing Afros, wearing cornrows and chanting James Brown's *"Say it loud. I'm Black, and I'm Proud"*.

However, Baltimore was a segregated city. Blacks segregated themselves by class. Every ethnicity had its own respective neighborhood. We knew after dark what neighborhoods we should not be caught in. The flip side of that was that I could never recall my family ever talking about white people or telling us to hate them. I only heard about segregation from my grandmother. But at Western, one of my white friends lived in the neighborhood we did not want to be caught in after dark. This was a new reality for me regarding race and relationships.

College was both a cultural and racial awakening for me. The campus was home to over 30,000 students, with less than 10% being Black. When it came to the physical sciences, I'd say we represented less than 2%. It was not unusual to be the only Black and only female in my classes. Little did I know that the same statistic would apply to the professional world as well.

After college, I entered the world with a Bachelor of Science in Electrical Engineering (BSEE) from a reputable societal school. Let us just be real, a majority white school. The career I had chosen was majority white males. During this time, Blacks were being represented in the various fields of engineering. However, we have scattered across the United States and, too often, the only one with that background in any respect for profit, nonprofit and governmental entities. The most important thing I learned in college was the true history of my Blackness.

There are two terms that I would like to introduce at the beginning of my journey. I heard a Black sister define these two things at a "Ted Conference": One is called, 'Professional Currency.' That is where you have someone in the room while you are not willing to advocate on your behalf. Or if you are in the room, having the courage to speak up for yourself.

The second is 'Personal Currency,' have your peers and coworkers advocate and substantiate your performance. As I see it, in a toxic and or hostile work environment, you need to learn, craft, strategize and cultivate these critical skills.

My first job was working at the National Institute of Health (NIH) in their Biomedical Engineering and Instrumentation Branch (BEIB). This was a group of very seasoned white male engineers with an outstanding electrical technician that was Black. Our job was to design and build instrumentation for research scientists. One such scientist was Dr. Anthony Fauci, of course much younger at that time. These guys saw no color or that I was a woman. They treated me with respect and genuinely wanted me to learn the craft of engineering. So, after leaving there to work in the defense industry unbeknownst, I was in for a very rude awakening. I mention this because not all workplaces are or can be toxic to us.

My first job in defense was after the space shuttle blew up, where there was a concerted effort to find engineers to go into quality. I was in Florida, where every other car on the road was a pick-up truck with a Confederate flag and a shotgun on a rack. While commuting to work, I became too afraid to look over at the cars passing on highway I-95, both North and South.

I was placed in a cubicle with an older white guy who tolerated me as a Black woman and engineer. Every day when I went into the office, he would check his watch. Daily, he would stand at the entrance of our cubicle watching me like a hawk while chain-smoking. I never knew what made him tick or what he did for the company. I now realize this was covert racism by the power of intimidation.

At some point, my boss hired another Black sister that looked like Phylicia Rashad on the Cosby Show, as my white peers told me. All of them had goo-goo eyes when she would come by to see me. Then another Black sister was hired. Now there were three of us. We collectively stuck together. We were intelligent, competent, and knowledgeable in our respective lanes. Though to my demise, I had fallen out of favor with my boss. It got so bad that I agonized about coming to work each day. I struggled to drive 66 miles each way every day. I could rarely complete a week. Being so young, I was unaware of the signs of anxiety, stress, and depression. I had gotten to the point while I laid in bed trying to sleep, asking God why was I even born?

I knew in my heart; God did not create me for the life I was currently living. From the world's perspective looking in, I had it good. I owned my first home at the age of 24, I was an engineer, and I worked at a major company. The truth of the matter was I was dying on the inside. My spirit was being crushed. So as a countermeasure, I started attending a bible study group at work. Then one of the sisters in the quality department invited me to home bible study groups.

Although it was a toxic work environment, I was able to perform my duties. As time progressed, I started reporting to another Director of Quality. The change was a breath of fresh air. He was encouraging and supportive. However, some issues were brewing behind the scenes with him and my previous boss. Do not get it twisted. Some politics go on between white males in a corporate environment too. I did not understand the depth of the issue until it came to my performance rating. My current boss rated me "above expectations" and we both signed the performance review. However, my previous boss went back and changed it to "meets." It was a nightmare. I went to HR, where a Black brother was the manager. He had me thinking it was my fault. You know, blaming the victim. When I took my case to the Equal Employment Opportunity Commission (EEOC), they did the same thing. In a filing with the EEOC, you had to put together your complaint. The results were binders of information and all-consuming because I wanted to fight for what was right. By the time I went through all of that, I was tired, stressed, felt hopeless, and completely burned out, and was done! I learned the hard way; sometimes, the processes that are there to protect us are smoke screens and are put in place to protect the company instead. Equally noted, Black people in positions that can help may find they are more for the company and themselves than not supporting or championing you.

One day as I was taking that 66-mile hike back home, I had an epiphany. I realized three things: "One, when I say I love God, I say I love myself; Two, when I say I love myself, I say I love God because He created me; Three, when I say, I love myself, I say I love ALL people, for how can I love people, if I don't love myself?" My whole life came crashing down before me as tears flowed from my eyes with relief. Having experienced such an emotional moment, I decided to rededicate my life to Jesus Christ. My mantra became, "seek ye first the Kingdom of God in His righteousness, and ALL these things shall be added unto you."

I had now set out to leave Florida. While attending a National Society of Black Engineers (NSBE) conference, I was recruited by this company to find minority engineers. At that time, I checked two boxes, I was Black, and I was a woman. Now some would think that was great, but believe me, it was a double-edged sword. What happens is that racism and sexism become a nexus that we must deal with and learn to navigate around. During this time, it was, "we want diversity; we just can't find any Black engineers."

I was hired to work for another large defense Fortune 500 company with tens of thousands of employees. When interviewing, I would take out my braids, but for this one, I wore them. After all, I had evolved to where I felt they should be hiring me for my qualifications, not because of my hairstyle. Many valuable lessons prepared me for taking this new job. I was equipped with the following: First, you needed to have a boss or someone in a position of authority to believe in you, and that will champion your competence, intelligence and not feel threatened- "professional currency." Second, you need to understand the landscape of who is for you and who is against you-"personal currency." You need to figure out where you want your career to go and plan on how you are going to get there.

Blacks at this company were scattered in different departments, one being human resources (HR). It was okay to be a manager in HR, but there were no Blacks in engineering or business development. This supported the common thought growing up: we were told what intelligence we were not born with and how we lacked the aptitude to be good in math, critical thinking, and communication. However, it was okay to be in support roles like working on the manufacturing floor and helping the manufacturing line. My new boss was a very brilliant white man who celebrated my diversity. He made sure I was trained in all the quality tools to do the job at hand. I now had begun to cultivate "professional currency." I was transparent about plans to go to school for law, a dream I had since college.

Do whatever it takes in continuing to grow your "personal currency." I walked that huge plant every day, from one function to another. I attended early morning production meetings to learn what was impacting production. I was raised to treat people the way that you wanted to be treated. Thus, I knew everybody on a first-name basis. I cared about them as a person, not for what they could do for me. There was at least one Black woman chemist, myself, and a host of others spread through the other departments. A Black forum was formed at the site to represent us collectively.

After learning and making my presence known, I grew a reputation. I had gained "professional currency." I was designated a "high performer" and promoted. Myself and the team won various awards for getting things done with an impact on production. But I wanted more. I had accessed the landscape and learned that to be a leader in this company. You had to get into the Project Management Office (PMO). I dared to dream!

The PMO had two requirements: One, you had to be a white male. Two, you had to have an engineering degree. Straight up covert racism. The PMO took the product from conception to delivery. They were held accountable for what they called then from "cradle to grave." They dealt directly with the Navy Admirals, Captains, 3rd party vendors, and lobbyists in DC. Thus, the PMO was your ascension to becoming a director, a Vice President (VP), and ultimately, a business unit president.

At one of our Black Forum's meetings, the VP of Engineering spoke to us and shared how the current President of the business unit had made his ascension in the PMO office. Well, well, well, I said to myself that is exactly what I would do. Wait, hold the phone. You have an engineering degree, but you are Black, and you are a woman. Remember that two-edged sword? Every time an opening for a project engineer became available, I would submit my application and resume. I never heard as little as a peep from anyone.

Being relentless and knowing that I met the qualifications, I would apply again and again with no response. During this same time, I was admitted to law school and started my journey to obtain a Juris Doctorate. It then became, *"What is it that you want to do, Dawn? Do you want to become a lawyer, or do you want to be an engineer?"* What do they say, "people without a vision shall perish?" Back then, I saw the relevance of obtaining a law degree even if the ultimate outcome was not becoming a lawyer. Yes, I made the ultimate sacrifice of working full time during the day and going to law school at night.

Always be willing to think "outside of the box." Look forward to five years and ask yourself where it is that you want to be. Remember, time waits for no one. You want to have something to show for the time you lived. Also, there will always be people who do not see what you see. Do not waste your time trying to convince them to see what they cannot imagine. Instead, be true to yourself and follow your heart towards your goal.

I had "professional currency" on my mind, given the overt racism in not having any doors opening for the PMO office, so I decided to set up a meeting with the business unit president. During this time, they had what you called the "chain of command." Which meant you could not meet with anyone above your level without letting your immediate boss know. Of course, I knew this, but in this case, I decided it was in my best interest not to inform him. At this time, my bosses had changed, and now I was reporting to this short old white guy, set in his ways regarding what they call unconscious bias today. So, he approached me after learning that I had initiated this meeting with the president. He asked what the meeting was for? Now, this was the same man who had informed me that there would be downsizing and I needed to find another job. So, I replied, *"I'd like to speak with him regarding my career."* I thought to myself, what did I have to lose? I was used to being told no, I had been designated a "high performer," and I possessed an electrical engineering degree. The worst thing that could happen is that he listened, and it went in one ear and came out the other. However, he agreed to meet with me.

Top executives sat on what they called "Executive Row." They had fine offices, wood furniture, and windows with a view. They even had the executive dining room where they did not eat the cafeteria food we had to eat. They had tables draped with table-cloths, silverware, stemware, and chefs to prepare their meals and serve them. Yes, this was what the "good ole boys" had at their disposal: the cream de la cream. Well, the time had come. I was on my way through the maze of buildings headed to executive row. Remember, "professional currency" allows you not to be afraid to speak up for yourself. I had no idea as to what to expect. Butterflies in my stomach, anticipation, but with confidence.

I was not going there to ask for any favorable treatment. I was going there to ask for the opportunity for a door to open that had constantly been closed. I had assembled my pertinent paper-work. In terms of preparing to present myself well, I had been an officer in Toastmasters and law school thus far had equipped me with what they called the IRAC (Issue, Rule, Analysis, and Conclusion). You get right to the point. What is the issue? I cannot get a door to open in the PMO. What is the rule? You need to have an engineering degree. What is the Analysis? You apply the facts to the rule. I had an engineering degree, which met the rule for entrance in the PMO. What is the conclusion? Given the analysis, I would like to be considered to become a project engineer in the PMO.

The President of the business unit was known to be a fine, reasonable, and humbled man. So, his assistant, a white woman, announced that I had arrived (no Black administrators were sup-porting these executives). He escorted me into his office and told me to have a seat. He sat directly across from me, not behind his desk that would have displayed a position of authority. I knew him. I had listened to him speak with our Black Forum, so I felt comfortable.

I began the conversation by reminding him that the VP had spoken about him at one of our meetings and shared his professional progression through the PMO office to now being the division's president. After learning this, I went on to state that I wanted to follow his path, but unfortunately, I had not been successful in getting an interview, although I had the qualifications.

After tentatively listening to me, he immediately got up, went to the phone, and called the current Director of the PMO office. This Director knew me because I had the reputation of solving production issues to get products out the door. He was also the person that never took me seriously about becoming a project engineer. And oh! By the way, he was mentored by the President of the division whom I was meeting with. The President told him he wanted him to give me an interview and find a position in the PMO. Right there, this man saw me for what I had brought to the table, what I had accomplished and saw fit to sponsor my entrance into the PMO. By the time I had concluded my meeting with him, I had a little pep in my step as I walked back through the halls of the buildings. Three different directors were already reaching out to me in the PMO for an interview. As they say, "Nothing beats a failure, but a try!"

"Personal Currency" includes getting assignments that are complex and will call attention to your skills and what you bring to the table. Remember, we must work twice as hard and be twice as good, just to get their attention. Never shy away from complexities that are affecting the bottom line. If you can, try to get these assignments since the bottom line is always REVENUE! I was given the most prominent problem of fielded equipment in the United States Navy fleet of ships. All ships! Frigates, Destroyers, Cruisers, and Aircraft Carriers. I was responsible for any problems with the Command-and-Control Data Systems on all ships. It was the customer's worst nightmare to fix. When introduced as the new project engineer taking over the problem, the room got quiet, and all eyes were on me. The room was full of about fifty white people, except for four Black sisters from the government who controlled the money!

I was placed in an office with another white guy who was a project engineer himself. We cultivated a good working relationship. It was him who had the problem but somehow could not solve it. At the Critical Reviews with the customers, they were comfortable with him even if he was not delivering. Somehow, I felt deep down inside I could use my "professional "and "personal currency" to solve this problem. I expanded my "personal currency" during those Critical Reviews by learning who all the players were. They were not just the folks at the plant who were important. It was the people who did the installations on all ships for upgrades and new product introduction and the integrators in Bath, Maine. In less than four months, the problem was solved, and the solution was headed to the entire fleet of naval ships for upgrades to be installed. Even in a hostile or toxic environment, there are good people. Good white people that see you for what you bring to the table and can deliver results. The bottom line is that everyone gets recognition when you are successful!

When presenting at the Critical Design Review with the customer, it no longer became my skin color or being a woman. They were elated with the results I presented. I had solved the problem. I was then promoted from project engineer to senior project engineer. My cube mate at the time asked, "How did you do it?" The problem was he managed from his desk. He had not cultivated any "personal currency." Given a chance or opportunity, we can always showcase our talents but still have obstacles.

At the same time, there was a transition of leadership in the PMO. They brought in this young white guy from another division with a finance background, not engineering. Say what? You will bring in a guy who did not have technical experience, who was as young as me, and you are going to what? Are you going to let him now run the entire PMO? He was white. He was young. He was good-looking and had charisma, but he was just like the old ones regarding unconscious bias. He accepted me; he had no choice. But he certainly was not going to champion my ascension in the PMO. That became crystal clear.

The customer liked him. The old and not so old guys in the PMO had no choice but to support him. They started to groom him for his new position. He relied heavily on their knowledge due to his lack of expertise in engineering and the functions of the PMO. He started scheduling one on ones with each member of the PMO. Mine was superficial. After all, I was Black, a woman, and I had something he did not have…an engineering degree!

There was a problem with funds following from the Navy. So upper management decided they would place someone in our field office in DC. They approached me since it was a group of Black sisters controlling the money. I was told to be the "eyes and ears" for the PMO. I connected with the U.S. government Navy contractor, who controlled everything between the Navy and the company. So, I got a leave of absence from law school (never told them), negotiated another promotion, and began my professional journey in DC.

The company's Washington administrator and I became extremely close. She possessed a long-standing relationship with the Navy contractor. Her responsibility was to deliver and receive important documents and signatures from the Navy to the company. Life was not a bed of roses being there. Why? The contractor had endorsed my assignment in DC. But there was one problem. He had an assistant who was a white woman who practically ran the office for him. It was well known. At the reviews, everyone kissed her ring, except the Black sisters. Management knew if they got in her ear, she would get into his ear. He made the final decision, but it was not without her input. Although she was intelligent and efficient, she disdained the Black sisters and later myself.

Those four Black sisters took no prisoners. They were intelligent, confident, knew their jobs, and were without fear. They had no problem ushering into the contractor's office in laying down the line as to when they would release the money and why. I think we call this RESPECT! They commanded respect from him and management back in California. His assistant was invisible to them. While there, I generated at least $9M in new business. They wanted me to stay and perform with no exit plan to get back to California. However, there was a problem. The assistant to the contractor had started to bad mouth me and my performance. This feedback got back to the young PMO director.

To be promoted to the next level below the director level, it had to go through the Executive team for consideration. It meant the PMO Director had to submit my name for consideration, who was using the feedback as a reason for not submitting me. Each quarter, the Director, VP, and President sat on the board. Now I had notoriety, but there was this lingering doubt by the seeds planted by the director. Remember, "professional currency" is someone that can advocate for you when you are not in the room.

The schedule had been set for the next meeting. We knew the date. "Personal currency" again came to bear. Remember the administrator in DC? Recall how we had formed a great relationship and how she was remarkably close to the contractor, the go-to person in DC, that controlled all activity for the Navy? Well, collectively, we developed a plan. The contractor got an Admiral's letter of Accommodation for my work and had it signed. The administrator got the letter and overnighted it directly to the President, Vice President, and cc'd to the young PMO director. The letter arrived the day of the deliberation. The PMO director saw that both the President and the Vice President got the letter as well. "Professional currency" resulted in a promotion to R&D PMO Manager III! My boss, who had advocated for me, came into my office after the decision and shook his head, and asked, "how did you do it?" I really cannot remember my response; all I know is I was smiling from ear to ear. I had won the day in the face of covert racism. Equally, I had also fulfilled that 5-year plan by graduating and earning my Juris Doctorate in Law!

I have worked in Research & Development (R&D) for the Government, Defense, Information Technology, Class III

Medical Device industries, Manufacturing of Pharmaceuticals, and my own consulting company that included being the target and product of racism in a toxic environment throughout my professional career of over 25 years. What I am here to say is that you are valuable. You were born with the intelligence that defies logic. You were created in His Image, and You are perfect in every way. Never give man control that he does not have. Find that inner strength to dare to imagine and Dare to Dream! Let your light shine, for the brightness always overcomes the darkness. Be love and give love. There will be many experiences that you must learn how to navigate. No compromise! You must stay Black and true to yourself and advocate in a white environment for basic acknowledgment, contribution, and advancement. Many will say that you cannot or tell you no, but do not let that be the end of your story. It is the beginning. You have nothing to prove, only to accomplish. As they say, "each one, teach one." We stand on the legacy of our great ancestors, their resilience, their inner strength to accomplish great things against all odds. Know that it is a "we" journey, not an "I" journey. Stand tall Black woman and Black man. Do not ever give in to the system but be a part of changing the system.

Remember, "the first shall be last, and the last shall be first."

An inspirational song growing up was Earth Wind and Fire's "Keep Your Head to the Sky" "*And He said, Keep Keep, your head to the sky…Keep… Keep your head to the sky…He gave me the will to be free….purpose to live is reality…hey and I found myself never alone chances came to make me strong…step right up and be a man cause yooou need faith to understand"…so we're saying- for you to hear…keep your head in face atmosphere…Keep your head to the sky…music fading.*"

Let me be as transparent as possible. If I did not say this, I would not be true to myself or you. When you meet me, you do not see what I do, nor what I have done. You meet me as a person. I am a Black woman of the Most High God! It is Him whom I put my trust in. It is Him that I pray for wisdom and strength every day. It is Him that gives me the peace that surpasses All understanding. When I look to the hills, I look to the hills from where my help comes, my help cometh from the Lord.

Yes, many nights, I have cried out to God, and He has heard my cry. I have seen Him make my enemies my footstool. I walk in the boldness of Him. I know He sits High, and He looks Low. I know the steps of a righteous man are ordered by God. I know His word! I trust His word! I do not give man power over me. I know He opens a door that no man can shut! I know promotion comes from God! For I serve a jealous God. Do not look to the right, nor to the left but keep your eyes stayed on Him. I am not here to preach to anyone. I am not here to convert anyone. I just want you to know that when you see a person cleaning your office or a Brother or Sister on the street that is in need. Acknowledge them, show respect to them. If they are in need, give it to them. But for the grace of God, there go I. So, my sisters and brothers, if you want to know the truth about my journey, I cannot take credit. For His word states, "if I be lifted up, I will draw all men unto me."

I'll conclude with a song from Charlie Wilson. *"Ain't a day go by that I don't try to thank the Lord up above…and if you wonder why I'm loving life…come close, and I'll tell you what's up…ask me how I'm doing…I'm blessed…yes…Living every moment, no regrets…smile upon my face I'm like oh! yes! I'm blessed, yes…I'm blessed, yes…repeat."*

6

New Frontiers, New Experiences, Same Racism

Kym Ali RN, MSN

I had an exciting opportunity to move to Qatar in 2014 to open the first Women's and Children's hospital. I had worked at various hospitals throughout the United States as a women's health nurse in numerous positions. However, now I had the chance to work as a Clinical Activation Consultant and collaborate with talented healthcare professionals worldwide. I felt overjoyed with excitement. Living overseas had always been a dream of mine since I was a child. Now my dream was becoming a reality.

I was responsible for hiring talent, developing policies and procedures, procuring equipment, workflow designs, and ensuring staff was adequately trained to provide safe patient care. It was a career opportunity I would never receive in the U.S. I viewed this project as my baby. I worked late, came in early, and even on weekends to ensure every system and process was optimized and staff had the resources, support, and knowledge to perform their jobs.

I received numerous accolades and recognition for my work, so I knew I would receive a leadership position when I applied. Unfortunately, I was denied the role after applying twice within the same year. The position went to a fair-skinned Pakistani British female who was underqualified and had a poor performance evaluation and multiple complaints about her work ethic. Once she assumed her new role, she plagiarized my work, removed me from projects, and alienated me against others.

The stress from her actions affected my health. I developed frequent colds, increased blood pressure and sleep deprivation which affected my mood and focus. I decided to take two weeks off on stress leave, praying that the situation would improve once I returned, but it didn't. I resigned two weeks later when an opportunity presented itself at a Fortune 500 company in Qatar.

The first month at the new job was delightful. Despite being a young, mastered, educated Black female on a team of 50-year-old Caucasian women with only a bachelor's degree, they were initially receptive. All except for one individual, a Caucasian woman from North Carolina, made fun of dark skin colors, curly hair textures, and heavy accents. From the team's reaction, you could tell that they were uncomfortable in her presence, but leadership did nothing to stop her. I had to engage with her since she was on my team, so I tried my best to minimize my interaction and ignore her comments even though they made me uncomfortable too.

Once I began to share new ideas that were favorable to clients, I became a threat. My team wanted me gone. Within one month, I went from being an excellent, bright, young go-getter to aggressive, insubordinate, and a thief.

Little did I know they were slowly building a case against me. The first warning sign was that I was labeled difficult. My preceptor instructed me to sit next to her in the office and not speak to other coworkers. A grown woman in her 30's didn't abide, and my manager wrote me up for not listening. I felt powerless and almost like a piece of property. It was demoralizing and embarrassing.

I emailed my line manager with my concerns hoping that she would see my side of the story and realize how absurd the situation was. My manager forwarded my email with my concerns to my preceptor. My preceptor privately approached me about the email the next day. Then she turned around and told my manager that I threatened her during our conversation. The final act was the most damaging emotionally and psychologically. I received an email with strict instructions to come to another office with a coworker; I was forced to drive my coworker in my vehicle to the main office as if I was a criminal. When I arrived at the new location, my manager called my coworker on her cell phone and fired me in front of her.

I later discovered what really happened. I was scheduled to go for training in another city. My friend knew I didn't have my company credit card and offered her's. My manager insisted that I use my preceptors' credit card and "get whatever I want while away." When I returned from my trip, my preceptor denied everything even though I had email correspondence and documents stating to get whatever I wanted because the company would reimburse the expenses. To solidify my termination, my coworkers went to the company's vice president to get his approval. It was a setup from the beginning.

I was told that, "they didn't want people like me working for their company and that my character was concerning." HR never investigated the allegation or spoke to me about what happened. I was terminated immediately and never heard from the company again. To make matters worse, I didn't even receive my entire salary for the month. Initially, I went into survival mode. I didn't have the luxury to mourn because I knew I needed to leave the country as soon as possible. My well-being depended on it. I was left in a foreign country, single, afraid and alone, and genuinely concerned for my safety. A travel ban was placed on me, so I couldn't leave Qatar until I paid all my debt.

If I were a Caucasian female, there would have been a formal investigation. However, because I was a Black female and adjectives such as angry, aggressive, and thief are commonly used to describe us, the story was believable. No one questioned it. I felt defeated, embarrassed, and ashamed. Despite my innocence, I didn't want anyone to know what happened because I didn't want my family and friends to believe it. It took me three months before I even told my mother what I had gone through in Qatar. I managed to safely exit the country three weeks later after paying off my debt.

My experience has led to paranoia in the work setting. I'm nervous if I receive an email from my boss or if people are meeting without me. I tell myself a story that they are planning to fire me, but I must constantly talk myself out of these negative thoughts because it's unhealthy and adds unnecessary stress.

I now own a business and use my platform to narrow the health disparities in communities of color and educate corporations on the advantages of equity and inclusion in the workplace. I am still in the healing process. Incorporating cognitive behavioral therapy and acknowledging my trauma was the first step in the journey. I made a conscious choice that I am going to be the victor, not the victim. Helping others share their trauma with systemic racism has also been highly therapeutic on my road to recovery.

Despite my ending, living overseas was a rewarding experience. I grew personally and professionally in ways I never imagined possible. I have traveled to over 65 countries, made friends with like-minded individuals from all over the world, and had once-in-a-lifetime experiences. I would encourage Black women to travel and expand their horizons but, if you are looking to leave the United States with the hopes of escaping racism, you may be disappointed.

Outcast

Nyrobi Wheeler, MBA, CPRW

Being only one of a few minorities within a predominantly white work environment for a non-profit organization has many challenges and frustrations, such as working harder than your white colleagues. I found myself having to go above and beyond what they asked me to do to prove myself in the job and organization. I had to work twice as hard and long as my white colleagues, which put me at my breaking point. I had previously worked for a certain non-profit organization as an AmeriCorps service member in the capacity of a volunteer coordinator, which evolved into a full-time position as an Assistant Staff Accountant after my service ended. In the beginning, I felt great about being offered the job—I was being promoted to accounting, an area I didn't have much experience in, but I was willing to step up to the challenge and learn.

I was the only Black employee in the accounting department,

which meant I always had to work harder than my co-workers to prove myself. This included coming into work at least a half-hour early every day to learn how to use the materials I needed to perform my job. It would help me reach performance goals by taking materials home, studying them over the weekend, and sometimes asking for extra help when needed. The person assigned to train me never showed any empathy. They constantly gave me a hard time, often putting me down when I did not get particular objectives down the first time.

When I accepted this new position, my supervisor stated that the objectives I would be learning in my new role would take at least six months, but my trainer had another agenda. After a few weeks on the job, I finally went to my supervisor about the way the trainer was treating me, and my supervisor stated, "I will speak to her about how she is treating you and since you are new to accounting, tell her to give you more time to learn the objectives." One day while I was at my desk, I overheard my trainer tell the supervisor, "I don't think she is going to work out because she is not learning the objectives fast enough." When I heard this, I felt betrayed and angry because my supervisor stated in the beginning that I would be given six months to learn all the materials to do my job successfully. What happened to the six months of training that we initially discussed that I would have to learn the materials thoroughly? Did the supervisor change her mind all of a sudden?

I had grown weary at this point. I didn't want to get out of bed to go to work anymore. I was depressed, pissed off, and felt unappreciated for my work and effort to learn this new position. I even took the time to speak with my previous supervisor at the organization, and as I sat crying in his office, I prayed I could go back and work in his department because I was so unhappy. I started to call in sick because I had begun to hate my job. Then, one day, I decided to turn my negative energy into being productive for myself, and I started looking for another job. I was tired of feeling stuck because I did not have another job to fall back on, but that was about to change. Yes, I had to remain there because I had to pay my bills. However, I was determined to find another position with a new organization that would appreciate my hard work, determination, and loyalty.

One day my supervisor called me into her office and stated, "I noticed that you have been coming in early almost every day. Please start coming into work at your regular time from now on." The next day, I got the courage to tell my supervisor I was tired of being mistreated and did not appreciate the favoritism that was going on, and before I knew it, I told her I was resigning. Her response to my resignation was, "Well, we took a chance on you." At that moment, I felt like I had just been kicked in the stomach. I was angrier than I'd ever been before. I immediately left her office, put all my belongings in my backpack, and left. Once I was outside, I began to cry.

After a few days, I felt like an enormous weight had been lifted off my shoulders. Yes, it was a huge relief to no longer have to work in that environment. Honestly, I did not realize just how much of an emotional toll the position and that workplace had taken on me. Now I was ready to start a new career where I would be appreciated for my hard work. After I left that organization, I had a difficult time obtaining another job, so I started my own online education consulting business, using my writing talents and skills in information technology by developing online self-paced courses in Spanish, French, Italian, and African American history for both children and professionals.

While focusing on my first small business, I was able to find a part-time position working as an Educator for another non-profit organization. The job was low-paying, but I needed it to have some income while I was still developing my business. I worked for the organization for two years, leaving once to work as an Optician. While working as an Optician, I had the same similar experiences while working in accounting. I would overhear the supervisors talking, saying things such as "I don't think she is going to last long in this position," even having one supervisor state in front of me that "I think you should quit and move on because you don't fit in with this organization." After only being there for a month, I went back to my educator job.

There were many issues in my educator job as well. I saw lots of favoritism, mainly when it came to family members working together in the organization. I was asked to open and close the center on several occasions, not feeling comfortable because I did not have the proper credentials. My supervisor stated that I only needed to take a couple more courses to be qualified as a high-level educator. That was soon pulled out from under me because after I took those classes, I was then told that I had to take additional classes. I did not have the money to take additional classes, especially not on the low pay while working part-time. I even asked my supervisor for full time, but she kept making excuses as to why that was not possible, stating "there is not enough money in the budget," but they continued to hire more workers. The whole two years that I was there, I started pursuing my Ph.D., but I had to quit since I did not have the resources to finish it—which I still regret.

I continued to look for full-time work and also worked on my small business at night and on the weekends. In July 2019, I was offered a full-time position at a community college working in human resources. I had worked for this institution many years ago, so I was happy about coming back. The staff in the department was completely different from the previous ones I had known. In the beginning, I loved going to the job and enjoyed interacting with previous colleagues and new ones. After a couple of months in the position, certain coworkers asked me to do things I wasn't fully trained on. I was also responsible for supervising student workers who would do any work that I could not handle, especially during the beginning of the month when I was responsible for preparing new and promoted employee documentation for board meetings.

I was also denied opportunities for advancement. For example, I wanted to do a Title IX training seminar. However, I was denied the opportunity because my supervisor stated, "I need you to stay and supervise the front desk." I found out that two of my white co-workers were allowed to go. I was also denied the chance to further my knowledge of human resources by having my tuition reimbursement forms misplaced by the supervisor. My supervisor claimed that I never turned in the documents, but I had copies of them on paper and by email.

When the COVID pandemic hit in March 2020, I started working from home. I was able to devote more time to working on my first small business, developing all of the online courses, and even creating e-books in the subject areas. I was also allowed to start teaching online for a private university in the Midwest, but I could not begin teaching officially until August because of the pandemic. In June 2020, my position at the college was furloughed and then formally terminated in September 2020. My supervisor called me on the phone to tell me that my job was terminated. She never said she was sorry that this happened to me or asked if I needed anything. She just hung up. I was furious but relieved at the same time.

As of recently, I was able to work for the college again, temporarily as an Upward Bound Instructor teaching online entrepreneurship courses to high school students. I had to go out to the college to pick up some "packages" that my new department had when it turned out that the old department had thrown all of my belongings into two used interoffice envelopes-I was so pissed off that they would be so inconsiderate of my personal belongings that I had to throw most of the stuff away because I did not know whose hands had been on them.

If you're wondering, yes, today I am happily pursuing my dream career of teaching business classes online for three colleges, being an author, and sharing my love of writing with others. I have also started my second small business, a resume writing consulting business, where I help professionals in the business and education field enhance their resumes and curriculum vitae. I also specialize in writing articles and e-books on career advice.

Being able to start two small businesses and work from home teaching online—I haven't been this happy in a long time. I have always been independent, and I love that I don't have to answer to a supervisor. I am free to be creative. My advice to any Black woman who finds herself in a toxic workplace is to keep pursuing your dreams. If you are unhappy in your professional or personal life, take the necessary steps to change whatever makes you feel unfulfilled, unappreciated, and down about yourself and your talents.

8

A Word From The Career Coach
How to Function In a
Toxic Workplace

Kersha T. Fortuné, M.A

*I*n a toxic work environment, you can experience feelings of isolation, frustration, anger, and sadness. These feelings can be amplified when you know you have been specifically targeted. Your emotions can affect your mental and physical well-being and your soul and spirit. As we navigate our careers, we can experience moments of uncertainty and doubt. We can feel overwhelmed as we attempt to find ways to get out of an undesirable situation and move either onto a new career or stay in our desired field. This environment can also silence you and create doubts about your accomplishments, skills, gifts, and talents; in fact, you may feel uncertain about a clear path to make another career move and may believe that all organizations behave in the same manner. In many cases, we think that the current situation may be safer than the unknown.

This is far from the truth. You are gifted and talented, and getting out of an unhealthy work environment is possible. First, you must believe that it is, and you must know your worth. Below are strategies and tips that you can begin to use today. How do I know? These strategies helped me work through an unhealthy work environment and eventually allowed me space to leave for better opportunities.

FIND YOUR TRIBE:

Find support from your tribe/network/friends (whatever you call it, find those folks for support!)

You do not have to endure this alone. Find individuals who will support you through this, allow you to vent, cry, yell, scream, kick, pray with you, pray for you and give you solid counsel on handling your situation. Although this situation can feel isolating, I will repeat it. *"You do not have to endure it alone."* This will help you have a place where you can express what's going on and remind you of who you are. Your tribe can look like family, spouse, life partners, friends, prayer partners, sports teammates, etc.

When I was in a toxic workplace, I was thankful for the folks there to support me. I reached out to my family, friends, and prayer warriors. They motivated and carried me through until the day of my resignation.

GET A THERAPIST:

A good therapist can help you unpack, support, and address the emotions and feelings you are experiencing and provide you with coping strategies. A good therapist will allow you to cry the entire session if you need to and truly express what you have been experiencing. Your mental health is equally important as your physical health. You deserve to have a judgment-free space where you can be excited to express your entire self. You can also check with HR to see if your company has an Employee Assistance Program that offers counseling at no charge.

CREATE A CAREER PLAN:

Have a plan in place whether you choose to stay or leave the organization:

If you can afford it, hire a career coach that will work with you and develop a career plan that will allow you to set realistic goals. Toxic work environments can cloud your brain with what you have accomplished. A career coach will help you assess and take inventory of your skills, strengths, and weaknesses and implement strategies to help you make that transition. Career coaches will also hold you accountable for the goals you set and keep you motivated.

You may be thinking, "what if I can't afford a career coach?" I am glad you asked. When I finally decided I would no longer stay in my current workplace, I prayed about it and started taking action while waiting on God to have the final say. I began to prepare for whatever was coming next. I had to shift my mindset from not knowing what skills I had to offer to believing that I had many skills. One of the first things I did was to update my resume. Depending on how long you have been in your role and/or field, you may not realize how much you have accomplished in the time you have been there. If you cannot afford a career coach, either pay someone to update your resume or begin to update the resume yourself. When updating your resume, you want your accomplishments to shine brightly. Below are questions you can begin to ask yourself:

- Did I implement any strategies or processes in my current role or at any point while working here?
- Did these strategies or processes save the company time and/or money? (Find out that amount, do not fudge the number?)

- Did I participate in any special projects and present it to any leadership level within the organization or to stakeholders?
- If you are a leader, under your leadership, did your team pass any audits, receive any special awards (city, state, regional, national awards) within your industry or field?
- Did I participate in any conferences and facilitate presentations, and/or represent the company at conferences?

These are just a few questions to get you started on updating your resume. You will begin to brainstorm even more and realize that you have accomplished a lot during your time, and you will be an asset to another organization or department.

IF YOU ARE SWITCHING FIELDS, BEGIN DOING RESEARCH:

Another tip, if you are considering switching to a new field, review and research skills needed and determine what can be transferred over. Please do not allow the toxicity of this situation to overshadow the achievements, skills, and talents. Industries may have their jargon, but some words have very similar meanings. For instance, the words: client, patient, student are all synonyms; the major difference is if an individual works in business, a medical setting, or in the education arena.

Once you identify your transferable skills, find out the specific software you have to learn. If this is a requirement, some organizations will train you in the software, or you can discover where courses are offered. Also, you may have foundational skills to learn the software easily, so do not let this hinder you from moving on with your job search.

REACH OUT TO YOUR NETWORK:

Begin to reach out to your network to learn of new opportunities. Conduct informational interviews to gain insight into what's trending in your desired field. Connect with others and listen to their career stories and how they overcame hurdles. Attend a virtual or in-person free networking event, listen to podcasts, check out social media pages of companies you are interested in.

WHAT TO DO WHILE STILL ON THE JOB:

If you decide to leave, start removing personal items. If you decide you no longer want to work for the company, you can start removing your personal items from your office space a little at a time. This includes any personal electronics, apps and programs that are on any computers, tablets, cell phones that you have utilized to do your job. This also consists of any files that belong to you, not the organization's information and/or property, as you may be held liable for removing the organization's information and/or property. Be discreet about what you are doing. This is not the time to bring out a packing box. You will be surprised how much digital information we have on our work electronics or in our office. If you are unsure of what that includes, this may be a good time to revisit your Human Resources Handbook and the contract you signed when initially hired. You will learn about your company's policies on harassment and what is considered organizational property versus your personal property. Also, even if you thought of an idea for your organization and the organization benefited, it is imperative you understand what you could be held liable and responsible for if removed. The employee Handbook will also help you understand the standard amount of time to provide the employer notice of your resignation and if and what benefits you are eligible for after you resign.

WAYS TO ADDRESS ANY EMPLOYMENT ISSUES:

Document, document, document! Document what is happening if you have not done this already. Write the details of incidents that occurred, time, date, and responses to what was said to you. Save any communication, emails, texts, voicemails. Write down dates, times, who was present when the incident happened, where, and the situation. This tip is crucial if you choose to move forward with reporting what is taking place to Human Resources or if anything legal arises. Be as specific as you can.

Confront the individual(s) contributing to the toxicity, but have a plan. If you have not done this, address the individual(s) who have created this toxic environment professionally. This is knowing what the HR (Human Resources) policy states against harassment. If needed, role-play with someone you trust can help you address any questions that may arise. Do not overthink it, just be the professional you are and address it.

When you confront the issue, aspects of the conversation may not go as planned, but the point is that you addressed it. Once it is over, do not forget to document what happened.

Caveat: I acknowledge it may be difficult for some to speak up in these situations, and not everyone may be in a space to do so, and that is all right. Be sure to document the situation so at least your voice is heard on paper.

TAKE CARE OF YOUR BODY AND FIND A WAY TO RELEASE THIS NEGATIVE ENERGY:

Our bodies are made to recognize when we are experiencing stress, whether it be good or bad. When in a toxic work environment, you may feel physical ailments linked to the environment you are working in. My blood pressure was higher than normal, and I was never in a relaxed state which affected my sleep pattern. During this time, I began walking more, and it allowed me space to commune with God even more. Another activity I found solace in was baking, which allowed me to focus on one task at a time, and I enjoyed every moment of it.

As I stated before, being in a toxic work environment can really affect your mind, body, soul, and spirit. Yet, there is hope to change this situation. If you choose to stay with your organization or move on to another, some of the tips mentioned here can give you food for thought and hopefully reignites the passion you once had for your career and hope that there are better opportunities. These career tips will allow you to see on paper how much you have accomplished in your organization.

This one situation or organization does not determine your worth, and it does not define your career identity. It is your right to feel safe and supported in your work environment. You are gifted, talented, and have skills that other organizations, industries, and/or departments need, but first, you must embrace your worth and believe that you can flourish.

Kersha T. Fortuné *is a Leadership Development Coach and Consultant and the founder and CEO of Kersha Fortuné Career Consulting Services, LLC.*

9

From Pet to Threat

Chaquita Gibson, DSW, LCSW

I chose this experience to share because it highlights how Black women are minimized when working in spaces with our white brothers and sisters. No one, at least no one wise, uses racial epithets anymore in the workplace. Instead, a bar is placed in front of Black women, and each time we try to jump over it, it is raised a little higher. It is an invisible yet intentional bar. As a Black woman, I have found that I have to have more education and experience than my White peers to compete for similar opportunities. As a Black woman, I have had to work twice as hard just to have a seat at the table and, in this case, be offered a chair and told to shut up. I am sharing my story because I want Black women to know that their experiences are real, they are not alone, it is not their fault, and they can still make incredible achievements.

The experience that I want to share out of the many is connected to my role as a social worker. It was my second year out of school, and I had started my career as a full-time social worker at a hospital. I intentionally looked for jobs at hospitals because I thought there would be more opportunities, including opportunities for advancement. I was working in an outpatient clinic providing therapy. I was so excited. This was what I considered to be the official start to my career. I transitioned from the field of education after 11 years of teaching, so I was not new to having a career, but I considered myself open to learning. I worked alongside a full-time nurse, full-time tech, and a medication provider that rotated clinics in this clinic setting. There was also a full-time nurse manager who was over the program, in addition to a social work manager. This new position allowed me to finally spread my wings and grow, or at least that is how it initially appeared. When I first started, I worked alongside an African-American nurse until she resigned for another position. A White nurse replaced her. The transition appeared smooth, we got along, and the environment continued to feel like we were a team. I felt like I could thrive and establish a reputation for myself as being a strong clinician. On a personal note, my experiences reinforced my belief that I was indeed in the right place. I was living out my dream, which made all of the sacrifices to get to this point worth it. My goal was to be an expert in the field of trauma. In my mind, I thought, "What better training ground than a major hospital network!"

Change soon came, and the program was moved to another location. That is when things began to fall apart. Although I was the sole provider of behavioral health therapy for the program at this location and an integral member of the team, I suddenly found myself being left out of decisions that impacted my work. The nurse who initially appeared supportive began to supplant me in decision-making. Instead of making decisions together, as a treatment team, I was told what I would do and what would happen. I was even left out of making decisions about what clients would be appropriate for the program. And although other clinicians at different locations were integral in making those decisions, I was not. I began to feel invisible. The decisions were often made solely by the nurse who consulted with the nurse manager, who was also white.

When I attempted to voice my opinions or provide input about program decisions, I was interrupted and talked over. I began to feel invisible. A tenet of the social work practice is valuing others, yet I was being devalued daily. I was responsible for helping countless clients learn to value themselves and set boundaries for how others value them. I felt demoralized, angered, and sad. I felt alone. As a woman, I have always prided myself in taking responsibility for my choices and taking ownership of the outcomes I desire. As a result, I tried to assert myself, speak up, and attempt to share on multiple instances. Each time I was shut down. With each encounter, I could feel myself shrinking on the inside. Although I don't know what the nurse and manager were thinking, they behaved as if that was how things were supposed to be. They went about it as if nothing was wrong; they did not skip a beat. They went about as if I was not there. They held conversations about the program outside of my office, in my face, and in the presence of other staff. When in my presence, they talked about improving the program census, never turning to even pretend like I was there. Their demeanor, always natural, methodical, and consistent. I could rely on being ignored and dismissed. I often reflected on the ethical responsibilities of nurses and other staff. I questioned myself at times whether they felt that those responsibilities applied to me. I asked whether they even cared or considered how I felt. Considering all of the evidence, I thought that they didn't. And it was not an unfamiliar experience. An experience common for Blacks in white culture of being treated like a pet then becoming a threat. I went from being an integral part of a team, receiving positive accolades from clients, training most incoming social workers, paying for and receiving advanced training to use evidence-based therapy with clients to being shut down daily and ignored.

In meetings, I struggled with surges of anxiety when I thought about speaking up. I felt anxious, but I also felt vulnerable. I thought that the nurse could do anything that she wanted. I began to second guess myself questioning whether it was me. I began to question whether I had anything of value to offer. This belief was in direct contradiction to everything I had worked hard to accomplish and to become. It was even in direct contradiction to the values espoused by leadership, yet with me, behaviors that contradicted the agency's values were allowed.

Being devalued became the norm in this environment, and it was accepted. When I was allowed to speak, my contributions were dismissed or ignored. I was treated as if I were incompetent, despite having two masters degrees. On one occasion, I chose to speak up despite the daily conditioning that reinforced that my voice didn't matter. I suggested to the program manager that locks be put on the doors leading to the staff offices as a safety measure. Again, I was ignored.

Soon after that, I was confronted by what appeared to be a male client that somehow got by lobby and lobby restroom checks by onsite security. This person hid in the men's restroom in the lobby and waited until after hours and the building had closed. He surprised me outside my office. I was sitting at my desk catching up on my notes when I saw something in the corner of my eye. I turned, and he was standing in the doorway. I was alone. There were two empty offices across from me, and the nurse's office was vacant and adjacent to mine. The call center was two steps outside of my office. When this happened, I could hear movement in the call center. However, no one came out to offer assistance or even see if I was okay. I am limited in how much I am sharing to protect the confidentiality of the client; however, I will say that it took some time before he agreed to leave. After the incident, I was shaken up. I reported the incident to the "team," including management. Again, I was ignored. It was only after a technician brought up the incident again to the same manager whom I had suggested to put a lock on the clinic doors that a lock was then put on the door. It was only after something happened to me that my input was considered, and even then, there was no acknowledgement because someone else had to bring it up. As a part of the team, the manager and nurse did not ask me if I was okay, and things went on like business as usual. This became a pattern—a pattern of openly not caring.

To offer further evidence, I cut my finger on a stack of hand-outs that I had just copied before going to a group one day. The cut was deeper than I thought I could get as a paper cut, but it was deep enough to cause a drip. I got up from my desk, holding my hand, walked over to the nurse's office where she had control over the first aid materials and told her I had cut my finger and asked for a band-aid. She told me no and said to me that the band-aids were only for the patients. I didn't push the issue or argue because, again, not caring was the norm. I did not report the nurse because this was a behavior pattern that was done in front of management and among management. Instead, I wrapped some tissue around my finger and went on to do my group meeting. When I had a break, I left the clinic and walked to a nearby store to purchase band-aids. I share this example to point out the culture in which I had to navigate. A culture in which I had to watch as other employees who did not look like me were given space to share their contributions and how they felt. I had to stand by and watch them receive an acknowledg-ment if they had a rough day or had a challenging client. I had to watch as others who did not look like me were treated like humans. I had to navigate a culture where the burden of commu-nicating and getting along with people who did not want to hear what I had to say was on me.

Despite these challenges, I persevered each day. Before I knew it, systematically over a year, I went from being an essential part of a program to feeling like a mule. When our program capac-ity exceeded what was appropriate, and I voiced my experience of feeling overwhelmed with facilitating such large groups of upwards of 15 or more patients, instead of being responsive and providing solutions or alternatives, my concerns were treated as if I were complaining. The response would be to talk about the importance of keeping the current group number, and management would move on. Nothing else would be said about it. Although it would come much later, at the time, there was no discussion about what would be considered appropriate. There was no consideration about burnout or my mental wellness as a professional. In meetings, the stares in the room were cold and unconcerned. There was never a friendly glance, a nod that let me know they were listening, nor a look of having any compassion towards me. I was ignored, and despite being on a "team," I felt alone. The stress from the workload and the lack of support from the "team" was disheartening. I came to learn that "team" meant them and not including me. A once recognized employee, I now found myself under constant scrutiny. As the therapist, if the program census dropped or a client did not complete the program, I was to blame. However, I was left out of the accolades if the program census was high and clients were successful somehow despite facilitating four therapy groups daily, providing individual therapy sessions, and case management. Emphasis was put on the accomplishments of the "team." In the course of two years, I had shrunken as a professional. I found myself having changed from being an enthusiastic, bubbly, passionate person to an isolated, withdrawn, quiet individual walking on eggshells. My input was not welcomed during day-to-day encounters, meetings, etc., and it was now the norm. After two years of being told what to do, I came to know what they thought was my "place." That was not being involved in team decisions, discussions, meetings, and so on. The feeling was inescapable.

I felt belittled, demeaned, and invisible. I began having trouble sleeping, and I had anxiety with every approaching encounter. I felt that they were empowered while I was disempowered. To make matters worse, this treatment permeated outside the confines of the team, and I found myself in situations with colleagues who exploited the opportunity. Although my perspective was not valued, I trained most new social workers being onboarded to the department. I actually enjoyed it. I wanted to make sure that I treated other professionals with respect and to show them support in ways that I had not received. I was also still hopeful at that point that things would get better.

One social worker whom I trained and supported during her onboarding turned out not to be an ally but an opponent. While I was a group facilitator at one program, she was a group facilitator in another sister program. I began to notice a shift in her attitude toward me. It started with her appearing helpful by pointing out errors or appearing interested in my outside training activities. I began having multiple encounters with this colleague where she would point out a misspelling or small error in a note. At first, I dismissed it and thought that she was trying to be helpful, but it became apparent that she was not trying either. When I would say, "Oh okay, thanks," and attempt to look up the note or ask for the client information so that I could correct it, she would withdraw and say that it was okay, she was just letting me know. She would rush to get off the phone when I persisted in getting the information so that I could take a look at what she was referencing. This colleague pointing out my errors became a pattern. It got to the point where I began to notice mistakes in other colleagues' notes and innocently asking whether they had received feedback from anyone about any errors in their notes. As I expected, no one I asked had, yet it appeared that only I deserved this type of unwanted attention from her. On another occasion, after being the lead among outpatient social workers in being trained on evidence-based techniques, I received a call from her asking about the training while she appeared interested. After baiting me with her false interest and questions about whether I had used the approach and who I had used the technique with, she asked me if I had permission from management to use EMDR with my clients. Upon initially accepting employment with my employer, it was conveyed that the agency supported evidence-based approaches. I had been trained in evidence-based practices, so it was appropriate to use. I found myself in most communications with her having to defend and or explain myself.

In yet another conversation, she inquired about what I was doing professionally, training, etc. she then let me know that she was fostering a child and said to me, "That's what I'm doing." The tone at which she said it was as if to gloat. It became a pattern with each encounter that I had with her that I was left shaded. There was never reciprocity or sincereness in asking how I was doing; it was always what I was doing, and what I was doing was being critiqued. It was at that moment that I realized that she was competing with me. I reflected on the impromptu conversations and realized that all of the interest in what I was doing was so she could outdo me. The shade did not end there; it continued until I started to feel like I was under a microscope, with every action being evaluated from a negative lens. When I supported clients with recommendations for additional time in treatment, which was allowed as long as it was supported clinically, that was critiqued. Her program at the time was struggling, and instead of focusing on professional improvement, focusing on her own team, or learning how to celebrate others, she was focused on critiquing and creating fault. Her focus on finding fault was with me despite having two other sister programs she could have focused on.

When she commented about her concerns about how long my clients were in my program, these same comments then were echoed at meetings by social work management. And when these comments were made, they were made as if there were things that should not have been happening despite program extensions not solely being my decision. Not to mention, before her comments and prior to her onboarding (being hired), clients readily received extensions in treatments as long as it was clinically appropriate, and there was never a problem.

I noticed that I was a part of a culture where criticizing your way to the top was the standard. Some would call this competition; however, a competition involves two people, often opponents, competing for something. I never oriented myself or thought to compete with my colleagues. There was no prize or reward to be gained trying to tear down the next professional. I became a social worker because I wanted to help, promote, heal, inspire, and help others to grow. Not to get distracted by competing with someone who was supposed to be there to help other people.

Nonetheless, I remained professional, focused on my clients, and focused on being a better person. I also made sure that I looked the part. And if things couldn't get worse. I found myself being criticized for wearing business attire to work. This same colleague of Asian descent and another white colleague made comments in my presence about me "outdressing the patients." A statement was also made about how it was inappropriate for me to wear suits to a group. I was at a loss for words. Here I was first, my work being criticized, and now my appearance being criticized by two women who were considerably younger than me. When I was in their presence, I could feel their negative energy and the stares of disapproval as if by dressing professionally for work, I was inappropriate. I felt offended and also angry at the same time. I felt offended because too many younger women who did not look like me were critiquing my attire, positioning themselves in a place of superiority over me as if it were their right to burden me with their contempt towards me or my clothing. This is a position that often White people feel that they have over Black people solely based on their right as "father knows best" or in this case, "mother knows best." Neither one of them were old enough to be my mother. When I interacted with these women, I never felt a sense of camaraderie or respect from them.

During this time, I found myself being profiled by a white occupational therapist who exploited the racial bias. Before the incidents with the nurse, I had not had any incidents with her before. One day she made known that she would record when I arrived and left the group. I had not experienced this before, and there were never any concerns about my time in or out of the group. Once she began taking notes, she commented to me after meeting with a client in my office between sessions about how I reported to my group a couple of minutes late. While walking out of my office, she would make herself visible in the hall and look at her watch while I was walking by. She made a habit of doing this as if to remind me that she was watching. After having these encounters with her, the nurse manager began making comments during multi-program team meetings about social work therapists being on time to group without clarifying or confirming what was actually happening. When she was there, I had clients tell me that she would ask questions about how they liked my groups, if it was helpful, and whether they had concerns. It is understandable for a professional to ask clients that they work with how things are going; however, it was done in a way that my clients felt necessary to inform me. Not to mention, she should have first assessed her own effectiveness. I say this because although I was unaware at the time, her job was on the line. All the while, she was bragging to me about how she was making upwards of $80,000 while I was making $55,000, practically supporting a whole program.

So I found myself in this situation again where "criticize your way to the top" was and still is the culture. In this culture, aggression, harassment, and bullying are looked down upon. At the same time, winning at all costs, which usually involves aggression, harassment, and bullying, is allowed. It appears that this practice is acceptable when one is Black. So, I began to contemplate how I could advocate for my clients or teach them to advocate if I could not take the risk of advocating for myself. There was a considerable risk. I feared losing my job, being retaliated on, and I feared that things would get worse. It was clear to me who had the power, and they used it freely to get and keep things their way.

I decided first to attempt to formally address my concerns with the relationship between the nurse and I. I requested a meeting with the nurse and the manager. I sent an email to my social work manager and requested that she join the meeting. I never heard a response back from the social work manager. I met with both the nurse and the program manager in an open-door meeting. The room was small, and the nurse and I were sitting next to each other with her on my right side and the manager sitting across from us at his desk. When I attempted to talk about my concerns with how I was being shut down in meetings with the nurse and not heard, I was interrupted and talked over by the nurse in the presence of the manager, who stated nothing and did not intervene. She began sarcastically apologizing while talking over me. The communication got so silly that she said that she would just be quiet from now on. All the while, I had not had a chance to say much. My intention for having the meeting wasn't to silence anyone but to have an opportunity to have a voice in a program that I dedicated much of my time with very little acknowledgment despite it being one of the most successful programs during my tenure there. Without a resolution, the manager requested that we go to the nurse's office to work things out for some odd reason. Although feeling dismissed again, I agreed, knowing that I could not make someone care about something or someone they actually did not care about.

The manager sat in his office two steps across from the nurse's office, peered at his computer screen, and never looked away. While attempting to follow up on the patients, which was one of our issues, she continued not to allow me to speak. She went on to slide toward me while sitting in her chair with wheels and got in my space. She said, "Am I giving you a chance to talk" sarcastically while turning her head to look at me. I felt offended by this, although this was the first time I had gotten consistent eye contact from her. I asked her to back away from me, and I left and went to my office. I decided to leave that day feeling that I had not accomplished anything.

When I accepted the position, I loved what I did, including my client population. I decided that day that I could not remain effective and continue to work on a team where camaraderie and teamwork were preached and not practiced. I did not attempt to report the issue to upper or executive management because nothing would be done. In addition, calling out bias and racism in the workplace has repercussions. I had already experienced the consequences of attempting to assert myself and attempting to get help from management. There was no follow-up from management, and again this was a part of a pattern of just not caring.

I decided not to file a complaint because I needed my job. I believed that if I reported anything to executive leadership or higher, they would just find a reason to get rid of me. I am not suggesting that others do the same. I am only sharing with you what I did because I felt I had too much to lose. I looked at America's report card on acknowledging when wrong has been done, taking responsibility for the wrong, and making a concerted effort to repair what has been broken and it didn't look good.

So I was not expecting anything different in the workplace. The same culture in society admonishes aggressive behavior yet permits aggressive behavior to accomplish a means to an end. Aggression is okay as long as you feel right or you can make yourself right. I experienced frequent, if not daily, microaggressions that served the purpose of conveying that I did not deserve to have a seat at the decision-making table. As a Black woman, I can work, make the organization money, but that's it.

It was okay to essentially mute someone because you felt right or you wanted to maintain control. In this case, this was only happening to me. Attempting to talk to the nurse that day was exhausting. The thought of trying to get someone to see how their behavior might be prejudicial was even more exhausting. This is not rocket science. If done to a white female employee, this behavior would have been a problem or raised concern. When muted, it opens your eyes to observe the relationships around you. I observed how they listened to each other intently, giving full eye contact, and acknowledged each other's ideas. No one walked out of the room on anyone when they were trying to speak, and no one cut the other person off, and if I did notice a slight interjection, they apologized. Although I am describing a communication pattern between two people, this permeated with other staff throughout the outpatient department.

I decided that it was not my responsibility to change, teach, show or educate people who choose to be ignorant. This is too much of a burden and a distraction. Just as I can educate myself, self-reflect on my own thoughts and behaviors, and be mindful of how I treat other people, so can they. After being minimized for almost two years, I had to go through building myself every day after being torn down. I frequently reminded myself of all that I accomplished and all that I had overcome. I decided to lead by example and not according to the examples provided. It was difficult to show compassion towards people who were not compassionate nor ethical with me. I reflected on why I became a social worker and how important it is for there to be people who look like me in this profession.

I focused on being an expert in my craft and not an expert in conflict. I have come to know about conflict and that although conflict can ignite change, it can also stunt growth and progress. In the end, I started a business and continued to pursue professional development. I decided not to allow others' behavior to define who I am or who I would become. I took control of the narrative about me, and I am writing my own story. I have a message for Black women like me and it is that you can still win even if you feel like the fight was lost.

10

Checkmate: From Trauma to Truth

Pia L. Scott, EdD, LPC, GCDF

*Y*ou write well, but you can't present well! You look scary! Everybody has that degree!" A former supervisor would make these comments to me. I previously worked in higher education in a role that required much more than what I expected. Everything I did was questioned, and when I tried to defend myself with proper evidence, I was not heard, as they did not care because of their perception of who I was. It has been a long journey working for others, and I never thought I would take the path of entrepreneurship. I started working when I was fifteen years old. When I first started working in corporate, I was working for the State of South Carolina, my first 'real' job out of college at the age of twenty-two. I was always willing to learn, grow, and understand my position as a professional.

I can genuinely say that I only had two great and professional supervisors who happened to be a white female and a Black male throughout my twenty-five years of working. I learned through their leadership the difference between management and genuine leadership. These two individuals were supportive, fought for me when needed, and held me accountable within my position.

Everything has a purpose, but sometimes it doesn't feel good. It doesn't feel good to be mistreated and constantly questioned, and your actions constantly scrutinized without justification or explanation. I was berated continuously, cursed at, had the phone hung up on me, yelled at, and once asked by another coworker, *"Are you only here to eat?"* while working an event. The incident was reported. However, nothing was done about it.

Organizations have their own culture, and I was only five months in and expected to know everything about this organization. There was so much red tape and processes that did not make sense or constantly changed, making it hard to keep track. However, once I learned the processes, it became much easier to navigate those challenges. Though, I still faced difficulties due to my supervisors' continuous harassment.

Even going to HR, the response was that this was an internal issue. Several instances caused me so much anxiety because I felt there was always something that I didn't do right, somebody I made upset, even though that was in their head, or always being judged. When I would ask my supervisor questions to get feedback to improve, there was never a response, or my supervisor would tell me that she didn't have the time. It became a no-win situation which caused me even more anxiety. I had situations where I was accused of doing or saying things that I never did or said. Once again, I tried to defend myself and never got the proper training from my supervisor that I should have received. I was always expected to perform at 100 percent because of my doctorate, while some of my colleagues were able to get away with murder. One colleague stated that she would be doing her homework at her events before the director, and nothing was said or done. There was blatant favoritism and racism within the department. During these events, I was being watched or asked to make copies even though I wasn't sure where to go because I did not work in that specific area, nor was it my event.

My work experiences were difficult because I was always over-qualified but treated as underqualified to do the work. I have been blatantly disrespected by supervisors, peers, and so on. I knew that it was time for me to move on and started the employment search process once again after three years of being in a toxic workplace culture and harassment. I experienced constant racism even in my job search. I could remember one interview I went on, and I was told that I was too young to have accomplished all that I did. In my second interview, the interviewer just stared at me as if I was on display. I came to a point where I was tired of other people's perspectives of what 'they' wanted me to do because they had the control or because they felt my accomplishments would overshadow their authority. Most of these experiences came from women. Despite these disappointments, I remember the import-ant people in my life.

My mother and late grandmother have always inspired me. I still remember my grandmother's words and what she would tell me about her childhood experiences during segregation. She would remind me that I had to be three times better and never forget where I came from. My mother always supports me, and she is not afraid to tell me when I am messing up and encourages me to remain humble. I was also inspired to become a business-woman and leader through my experiences in the workplace and encouragement by many people in leadership roles to break into entrepreneurship. I have met several different professional men and women throughout my travels to various conferences, events, and organizations and these individuals continue to support me.

I have also met some amazing professionals with much wisdom, truth, power, and love throughout my career. My mentors, Dr. Porter, Pittman, Shell, Driggers, and the Staten's, have been incredible. I feed off of their energy. I am iron being sharpened by iron, and I am genuinely grateful for the inspiration. These individuals have so much expertise and resiliency in their own stories. They inspired me because of the different levels of wisdom and knowledge that I gain to grow, learn, and apply in my life and business. I decided to leave higher education and pursue my dream of being an entrepreneur. I no longer wanted to ask for permission to be me.

The trauma I experienced was something that I needed to go through to find the truth in my purpose. All of these experiences led to some positive outcomes as well. The truth is, I was able to help thousands of students with career development, make connections with departments within the organization and community, and gain skills that I can use in my own business as I continue to serve. I got what I needed while I was in the previous role. I didn't realize that those same connections and experiences would propel me into entrepreneurship and becoming the CEO of my own coaching and consulting group where I now inspire and empower people of color and their allies in overcoming challenges – checkmate!

11

The Silence of the Soil

Danne Smith Mathis

*A*geism. The reality is, when you enter what is known as a "protected class," you are a target. This is one of the most challenging classes for a Black woman to attend in Corporate America. You are usually the oldest student in the class, and the dynamics of generational diversity within the workforce are not part of the corporate syllabus. This often leads to younger supervisors with power over someone whom they rarely respect.

Micro-aggression. The fact is that when you are a threat to a colleague because of their lack of self-esteem, or better yet because you are simply better at something than them, you are a target of their professionally transmitted anger. You are bait and disposable. And if you are a Black woman, while seen as a pillar of strength and resourcefulness during interviews, even your years of stellar performance reviews afterward become like sunken debris in a sea of forged failure.

Racism. The truth is that racism not only exists but also permeates the soil of the souls of the majority to varying degrees at the expense of the minority to a large degree. It germinates in the hearts of too many whose construct is designed by architects of hate. They loathe what they do not know or understand and purpose not to. For Black women, racism is the thing that defines them as angry…the thing that desires to quiet their confident demeanor. To silence their commanding respectfulness. To eliminate their continued tenacity despite the false narratives that echo in their minds.

Sexism and Harassment. Women have always been the target of untamed eyes because men are visual and usually in control. Therefore, men demand women to carry themselves in a specific manner for acceptance in every situation and environment, situations, and environments men typically control. Control that forces a conducive climate to rules they make and skirt. When you do not perform to the likings of others' standards, they will make your life a living hell that spreads like cancer, and you won't know it is even there as it silently slays you until it's too late.

Gaslighting. Supervisors and peers with some level of planned-for-a-time authority over you will collaborate with others who only know what they hear about you to gain others' votes to join them in making a case against you. Often, this case presents a narrative so convincing you will think you are crazy, wrong, and at fault for all the discussions that all of a sudden begin to take place because you are "difficult to control." This is the art of gaslighting. This is the necessity of narcissism, a characteristic that even women of lesser color in Corporate America use to displace their colleagues of color when they suffer from their own ineptness.

Tone Policing. If you are a Black woman, your supervisors and others in a position to determine your career path will listen more intently to your voice, not so you can be heard. Your recommendations aren't taken seriously, but mainly to listen for that distinct tone that accompanies the soul of a Black woman. This tone bespeaks her confidence, stamina, intellect, and character, all of which grew out of the soil of the struggles of her ancestors. The tone that makes them uncomfortable because they cannot determine her next move...a move rooted in the legacy of the spirit of her foremothers who were forced to leave less than desirable living conditions. A move that required soul-searching in silence until it was time to say "checkmate" like Harriet Tubman quietly escaping the lies of the land.

These definitions represent all-too-familiar experiences of women and, most often, women of color. They are the seeds planted by those who own the gardens of corporate America-those who farm the land of inequity to capitalize on the labor of those they hire who they inevitably seek to marginalize and eliminate from the playing field.

Working in a toxic environment impacted my health and confidence as an employee and as a human being. Such an environment affected my ability to think clearly and continue as a thought leader. It negatively affected my ability to perform well in my position. Thus, I invariably second-guessed myself on matters of professional expertise that I would have never questioned prior to being placed into such an environment.

When you work in a toxic environment, your employer cuts the company's nose to spite its face. It loses its sense of smell for those who enter its corporate hallways with the intention of flushing out those with whom they have a close reporting relationship to reduce them to something less than human because of their own personal and professional insecurities.

Ultimately, a company defaces its property—you—when it creates a toxic workspace unknowingly as it employees those without sensitivity. It allows managers and other direct supervisors to write the graffiti of subtly penned lies onto the whiteboard of the minds of others for whom they prescribe for an incurable illness.

In turn, this disease spreads like the odor scent of a dead animal—a smell that permeates the corporate air, until finally, it enters the mental spaces of your existence where you decidedly dedicated yourself wholly to the corporate vision and mission with integrity and intellect- a standard of extra expectancy from people of color imposed by those who brought the crayons to the table in the first place.

As a Black woman, I knew ultimately, it was my Black self in corporate America some seemed to despise. Therein was the problem, not I and not Corporate America per se, but the poisonous tentacles of those it allowed to infiltrate its purpose.

12

The Narrative

Cat Rayner, DHA, MSW, MPH, LCSW

STORYTELLING

So often, women of color can be the victim of the dominant culture, a psychologically unsafe space. The dominant culture consists of those individuals of Caucasian ancestry in the workplace. This modern-day victimization appears in the form of telling a story. As we know, in the basic story, the characters must have a position. Often, one is the victim, and one is the villain. For women of color, there is no choice in which role she will play in the story. The system is designed for only one position, which is that of the villain. An attempt to stray from the role will be dismissed and discredited. By virtue of skin color, there is no refuge or hiding from the position. For those of us with a darker skin hue, the expectations of the villain are placed upon us from the dominant culture. This culture is based on the social construct of race.

There is no shelter or hiding in the workplace. As a Clinical Social Worker, I have experienced this lack of reprieve from the outer layers of my skin tone. My hair texture does not offer any relief as well. This can easily be an area of focus at the most formal of meetings. The dominant culture's curiosity is to address the most basic microaggression that a woman of color can be subjected to. This is a full-blown chapter in the story of frequent encounters and questions about a woman of color's hair. Please be ready, as this is the most foundational experience in the script. The narrative is designed for your reaction to the violations of personal space regarding hair.

The dominant culture older generations benefited from teaching their young how to perpetuate the long-standing benefits of systemic racism. Within the underrepresented culture, there remains hope to avoid the cycle of racial trauma for future generations to be inclusive and accepting of all. Despite the cultural advances of future generations, the narrative of the workplace remains the same for women of color. The broader organizational culture will not allow another construct to exist other than race. Other minorities may hide or blend into the dominant culture. Yet, the narrative will remain the same for women of color.

Throughout my career, I have experienced the narrative written by others, creating situations placing me on defense. I have been the victim of workplace harassment and bullying based upon the narrative that others made. The role of the villain is a tough one to overcome, especially when the office group thinks to target the woman of color. There have been opportunists who've taken advantage of my token status and exploited it fully. Furthermore, these individuals have used their privilege as a means to slander, defame, and discredit. There is no thought or attention given to harassing a woman of color, for the dominant culture is aware that no one perceives her as a victim. Remember, the role is that of a villain for the woman of color in the workplace. Other monitories joined in the workplace bullying, creating great psychological distress and anxiety. At times, other social workers were actively involved in contributing to my demise. Despite these barriers and behaviors of others, I overcame and changed the narrative. As a result of this resiliency, I can support others and foster a positive work culture.

WHAT IS THE NARRATIVE?

In an organization, a person of color must anticipate and expect a narrative to be written. There is no choice whether the individual wants to have a narrative as it has already been constructed. At least, this has been my experience in the workforce, where a narrative is written based on falsehood and allegations. The allegations have been a direct attack on my character. This includes the stereotypical angry Black woman, where each encounter is an emotionally charged experience rather than a difference in communication style.

Recently a male coworker wrote a statement that I was "going to get another co-worker." The statement was clearly false, but once he spoke the falsehood, it became the truth. In the past, I would just ignore the issue and just wait for things to settle down. However, I reported the concern to my supervisor on this occasion, which led to an investigation. The outcome was that the statement was not true. Despite the finding, no one in leadership apologized for my experience. There was no empathy or sympathy given. The individual did not experience any adverse or recourse for his actions. When I am in negotiations that result in a contrasting point of view, it is met with an emotional description of my position and decision-making. Often in meetings with my supervisor, there is reference to my behavior or mannerism. This occurs on such a frequent basis, I have become immune to discussions and feedback. The difference is that I have begun to use the opportunity to define microaggressions and microinsults. The most recent was when I gave a presentation to senior leadership. My supervisor stated, "You speak so well." This gave the assumption that I do not speak well on a regular basis.

It is well known that as women of color, the negative labels come easily from those who oppose us. The opposition can come from a simple workplace disagreement or a denial of a request. The narrative involves the bullies and the mob working together to write a narrative rooted in the racial construct embedded in the institutions.

Approximately ten years ago, a supervisor worked tirelessly to chip away at my self-esteem early in my career. I was an upcoming social worker learning how to implement a program to serve individuals with severe mental illness. With each challenge thrown my way, I was able to overcome and be successful. The challenges consisted of hiring employees with behavioral problems. Also, this included my immediate supervisor becoming threatening towards me in front of a group of peers. The two females worked hard to tarnish my reputation and label me in the organization. This included having other peers turn against me and isolate me from others. The psychological abuse was taxing on a daily basis. There was intentional targeting and bullying that led to the supervisor being investigated by the other people of color and I. The supervisor, on numerous occasions, verbally threatened to tell me, "You don't have what it takes to be a supervisor." At this time, I wasn't even attempting to be a supervisor or a leader in the agency. I was known for being a change agent and being able to execute. My ability to implement programs and lead people received the attention of senior leadership. As a result, I became a target of the two supervisors. Eventually, I was able to transfer from the agency and continue on my career path.

As a Clinical Social Worker, there can be a lack of equity across the system industries of education, healthcare, business, or non-profit. When opportunities are given to those of color, it is perceived as a need to satisfy a diversity requirement without regard for the candidates' ability to operate on merit. When opportunities are present to expand or for growth assignments, they will be denied if they do not fit the narrative.

The narrative is an invisible constraint in which the manner that this is challenged is of the most importance. Unwritten rules of engagement and pitfalls must be avoided to sustain a viable career and livelihood. When an individual strives towards greatness and optimal job performance, there are many additional stressors. Those with privilege are aware of this luxury and have used the societal advantage for personal gains and at the expense of other individuals. Often, people of color are often the ones to lose. The benefit and gain of the dominant group is to give great attention to developing the narrative. The group will not stop at any cost to keep the focus and pressure on the woman of color.

There is a way to challenge and change the narrative. This begins with an awareness that the narrative even exists. Once you realize that there is a narrative written about every individual of color upon arrival in the organization. Then the work begins to challenge every construct about individuals of color, including social workers. Advocacy is a core value that one must engage in with social justice. This includes being in a position to advocate for a standard of professionalism and equitable treatment. This includes the expectation that other peers would not engage in the negative narrative for taking a stance. For standing up for a social injustice that is rooted in systemic negativity.

SO, WRITE YOUR OWN NARRATIVE

The narrative themes tend to be negative descriptives or adjectives that focus on conduct in the workplace. The behaviors that are consistent and congruent with culture are viewed as unwanted behavior. If the individual has a position of authority, great attention to those opposed to women of color will be given to discredit. I can recall my supervisor chastising me for using my hands while I spoke to others. The accusation that the use of hands was considered a gesture and threatening. I politely pointed out to her that she was using her hands in that conversation. My statement did not help and only added gasoline to a raging fire. Her rage was driven by the narrative that I had a conduct problem, that I was deficient and could not collaborate or work with others. I found that the few individuals that opposed my authority were given great power and a voice to communicate lies about me. Talking with your hands may be considered a form of non-verbal communication or a form of cultural expression. However, there is usually nothing considered negative if an individual is using their hands while speaking.

Other narratives tend to focus on labeling any slight behavior into a negative perspective. The dominant culture creates the situation for opposition and then uses this as an advantage. A woman of color in the workplace can expect to be labeled. This will only contribute to victimization and psychological distress. There will be no rescue from workplace bullying. There will be no safe space or place to hide from the suffering.

Essentially, their labels will build up and accumulate into a series of adverse stories. Eventually, your reputation will fit the narrative of being difficult, oppositional, defiant, and not a team player. Each day your intellect and abilities will be challenged or questioned. Your integrity will be attacked with no one to stand up—with a high probability of the labels being validated by the dominant group. At times, an ally may attempt to stand up only to have the group turn and attack. The victim will suffer in silence a series of microaggressions and microinsults. Baseless accusations related to conduct and behavior will persist within the organization. There will be no escape from the narrative written by others.

There can be a way to work with others to change the narrative systematically. There is hope on how to change the narrative written by others. This begins with each interaction ensuring that respect and kindness are promoted, not enabling the dominant culture to lead the discussion, and making the culture aware. Often, I have very open discussions of my experiences and how others have treated me. I take great effort to change the narrative by taking a passive, less threatening approach. I discuss that narrative and challenge every interaction that threatens my actual experience. If I am attacked or harassed, I openly discuss my perception and viewpoint. I do not accept unwanted behaviors or communication. I expect authentic truth and communication.

Unfortunately, I have encountered fellow social workers not upholding the Code of Ethics related to social injustice and equality in the workplace. I strive to have open dialogue on how to change these negative narratives and provide further opportunities for future social workers. This is how change evolves in the unwritten script. In the workplace, challenging counterproductive behavior continues the systemic practice that undermines the woman of color.

- Keep an open dialogue.
- Challenge behaviors that are unwanted and unwelcome; this includes labeling your behavior in a negative manner.
- Report unwanted interactions such as verbal and psychological abuse to the designated department in the workplace.
- Speak up about the realities in the workplace that are unsafe.
- Use allies to foster and promote a positive narrative
- Defy the construct of race
- Share your perspective in an authentic manner
- Refuse to accept the script or narrative that is negative

13

All My Life, I Had To Fight!

Meleaha R. Glapion, MPA

I believe the very plight of being a BLACK WOMAN in America was captured best by Alice Walker's The Color Purple — "*All my life I had to fight! I had to fight my daddy. I had to fight my uncles. I had to fight my brothers. A girl child ain't safe in a family of mens, but I ain't never thought I'd have to fight in my own house!*"

Even today, my mother proudly shares with others how I, Meleaha Ruth Glapion, "miraculously fought against doctors saying my birth survival rate was 1% and that the very timing of my birth interrupted The Young and The Restless." Just a week shy from turning forty years of age, for over the last decade, I continue to "fight the good fight" and have pro se filed a total of three, going on four, Title VII federal civil lawsuits against systemic employment racial discrimination and retaliation, by local and federal government agencies.

December 1, 1955, a Black American civil rights activist, whom the U.S. Congress called "the first lady of civil rights," was arrested for civil disobedience, jailed, and criminally charged with "REFUSAL TO COMPLY WITH PROPER ORDER" for violating a white male bus driver's orders to give up her seat in the colored section after the white section was filled, to a white man. It was not because Mrs. Rosa Parks was tired physically or any more tired than she usually was at the end of a working day; she was — tired of giving in.

January 27, 2012, I, Meleaha Ruth Glapion "REFUSED TO COMPLY WITH ORDER" (notice charge was framed without prima facie element "proper") of a "white Mexican" male's (his sworn deposition self-identification) order to complete an involuntary detail to an unfavorable program area. I was the only employee ordered to perform such and the only Black American female within Field Policy and Management's Regional Office of six states. I was immediately placed on emergency suspension, administrative leave, escorted out of the building by three men (one-armed security), escorted back into the building on March 15th and March 20, 2012, by armed security to prepare and give removal replies, would undergo eight hours of an EEOC deposition on March 27, 2012, and eventually removed on March 30, 2012, from my position and federal service according to 5 C.F.R. Part 752 for "misconduct." It was not because I held a disregard to my obligation as an employee of the federal government; or that I was without the familiarity of the unfavorable program area where they ordered me to be detailed. Like my sorority sister, Mrs. Rosa Parks — I was tired of giving in what I reasonably opposed and believed was against anti-discrimination laws by the very federal agency tasked with preventing housing discrimination.

Fast forward to July 18, 2018, a date that I will never forget. With less than two years into my career as an Emergency Response Team Social Caseworker with the City and County of Denver Department of Human Services and two months after returning from maternity leave for my first child, I was retaliatory assigned a "near-fatality, fatality" case of a two-year-old Black child who had accidentally drowned in the backyard pool of her maternal great grandfather. Up until this date, I had never been assigned a "near-fatality, fatality" case. Care and due diligence of possessing a higher education from law and graduate school, with previous work experiences as security, Crisis Prevention Intervention ("CPI") of at-risk adolescent youth, human services, and federal management… My skills and strengths as a Social Worker were safely responding, documenting, and capturing the truth.

I was retaliatory assigned to this case because when the clock turned 4:30 PM (after hours), the white-divorced Social Caseworker Supervisor deemed her own immediate departure from the office "to go out on a date" more critical.[1] Cultural consideration of my being assigned the case was also correlated to being Black, and personal familiarity with the underserved neighborhood wherein the child and her family resided. In short and unambiguously applicable, the director of the county department is to be immediately notified of any egregious incidents of abuse and/or neglect, near fatalities, or child fatalities, and the director of the county department designates an individual(s) who will be responsible for assessing the egregious incident of abuse and/or neglect, near fatality or fatality.[2] In my case, the director of the country department was another white woman who testified herself that she was not immediately notified, nor did she designate that I would be responsible for assessing the near fatality or fatality. Denver Department of Human Services Child Welfare Division's all white "leadership" (what I rightfully deemed, and whistle blew on October 30, 2018, as being "dictatorship") failed to follow controlling legal authorities outlined by Volume VII, and to make matters worse, covered and concealed the white-divorced Social Caseworker Supervisor criminally falsifying the public records[3] of the two-year-old Black child who had accidentally drowned in the backyard pool of her great maternal grandfather, with racial animus to remove her two surviving brother siblings from their Black home, and to wrongfully terminate me from what I had considered to be, at the time, a rewarding career … Matters have gone before several different tribunals including: the federal Equal Employment Opportunity Commission (Charge Nos. 541-2019-02097 AND 541-2021-00132); City and County of Denver Career Service Hearing Office and Board (direct appeal numbers 73-18, 76-18, and 80-18); the United States District Court District of Colorado (Glapion-Pressley v. Denver Department Human Services, 1:19-cv-02806-RPM); Colorado Department of Labor and Employment to then Industrial Claim Appeals Office (Docket Number 1342-2019); and are pending before District Court for Denver, County, Colorado (Case number 2020CV405); and U.S. Court of Appeals for the Tenth Circuit (Case No. 21-1223).

I am thankful that I was granted assistance from a pro bono attorney whom I have referred to as "a real-life Atticus Finch"[4] for the aforementioned third federal Title VII case number 1:19-cv-02806-RPM against Denver Human Services. However, grave disgust and dismay came when the white male magistrate, who dismissed my first two federal Title VII Civil Actions dating back to 2014 (14-CV-03237-MEH AND 14-CV-03236) , recommended to the presiding Black male judge, dismissal per technicality of my formal pro se EEOC complaint making an express reference to 28 U.S.C. § 1746 by chapter & verse and not "perfected" with three explicit words "penalty of perjury."[5] Despite my May 14, 2019, verified EEOC intake questionnaire being sworn under penalty of perjury, along with supportive legal arguments of 29 C.F.R. §1601.12(b), on October 14, 2020, recommended dismissal was ordered.[6] On May 28, 2021, the Rule 60 relief from judgment order motion to reopen my case was denied.[7]

Although I was to be "protected" as a whistleblower and for engaging in protected activities in temporal proximity of adverse actions, because history is written by its oppressor, upon perform-ing an internet search of my name, you will see how I have been publicly "BLACK-BALLED" from the "SNOW-BALLING" of harmful "WHITE-LIES" (emphasis with appropriate color con-notations). What you won't see is — how — before the Merit System Protection Board ("MSPB"), four federal white privileged employment attorneys' went against one pro se ME-leaha; my traveling to Florida and Texas to conduct depositions of named discriminating responsible management officials who "resigned" or "retired" and fled out of state during proceedings; my reject-ing offered employment discrimination settlements for $25,000 and $100,000 pale in comparison "to making me whole"; my not consenting to the white male magistrate named in all of my federal Title VII suits, especially when I pro se filed a motion for his recusal and always doubted his impartiality, even more so when at the first scheduling conference, he took the crying white-male U.S. Attorney that represented the discriminating employer, back into his private chambers, to console him over "alleged personal matters" before proceedings wherein he auto-matically granted his verbal plea for a non-conferred extension of late and not produced discovery evidence; the city administrative hearing officer plotting his abuse of authority in rulings and five days of hearings, which he closed to the public, and my proceed-ing pro se against the discriminative employer's white- female lead attorney and white-male co-counsel; my loved ones' support and struggle with vicarious trauma from witnessing my severe holistic (physical, mental, emotional, financial, spiritual) suffer-ing; courageous others' being retaliated against for furnishing notarized affidavits or declarations or testifying as a witness that I subpoenaed; and prior to present trying times of COVID-19 matched with "reignited racial tensions" — government agents targeting to wrongfully remove black children from their home and black women, not just myself, from their careers' and ulti-mately their homes — MATTERS!

Understandably, when and if anyone "exhausts all administra-tive remedies" for illegal discrimination and/or retaliation claims against any employer, inevitably, they will "never be made whole," become exhausted, and/or worse, extinct. While I was uncertain if I would continue with my second U.S. Court of Appeals for the Tenth Circuit (Case No. 21-1223, against Denver Human Services) along with three other separate pending lawsuits, unbeknownst at the time I submitted herein chapter, my position as the first Director of Policy and Advocacy at The Center for African American Health would be eliminated.[8] Hence, I am more confident that God, the judge of all judges, has the final judgment and that I have been better equipped and positioned to serve and "fight the good fight" as a limited liability company Sole Proprietor of PRO SE (Person Representing Others' § (&) Self Equality) LLC. Most importantly, as a strong surviving[9] black mother to the only justice I personally know — my three-year-old son, rightfully named MARSHALL.

NOTES

[1]Testified to by myself and two other Emergency Response Team Social Caseworkers who were subpoenaed as witnesses, identified as Black or African American, before the City and County of Denver Career Service Hearing Office and by their written sworn affidavits. *See Glapion-Pressley v. Denver Department Human Services,* 1:19-cv-02806, and/or EEOC Charge No. 19-CV-02806.

[2]Controlling legal authorities outlined by Volume VII Code of Colorado Regulations (CCR) Social Services Rules (SSR) 12 CCR 2509-2. Commonly referred to as "Vol. VII" and/or "Colorado Children's Code".

[3]Colorado's Statewide Automated Child Welfare Information System, known and referred to as "TRAILS"; which is only accessible by/through certified and authorized users to the Colorado Department of Human Services Enterprise Portal per protections by HIPPA under the authority of the U.S. Department of Health and Human Services.

[4]Harper Lee's — To Kill a Mockingbird.

[5]The Due Process clauses of the U.S. Constitution and pursuant to 28 U.S Code Sect.455(a-b) — "Any justice, judge, or magistrate judge of the United States shall disqualify himself in any proceeding in which his impartiality might reasonably be questioned. He shall also disqualify himself in the following circumstances: Where he has a personal bias or prejudice concerning a party."

[6]Disparity of Black jurors, attorneys, magistrates, and judges, shatter there truly ever being a "justice system".

[7]Pseudonyms were not necessary in composing and maximizing moments of my contributing chapter. All case numbers were/are public record and may be of assistance to others. Further, I have never signed a non-disclosure act.

[8]No less than a week after my position elimination, another Black woman with a paralegal background who complained of "hostile work environment of nepotism, favoritism, and sexism..." — involuntarily resigned. Around the same time, I was forwarded and re-awakened by Author Dr. Carey Yazeed's YouTube: #CarChronicles, *"Why Black Women Hurt Other Black Women, Internalized Oppression..."*

[9]*"I too never thought I'd have to fight in my own house!"* Thankfully, God's glory comes with PRO SE prevalence of — being granted a permanent protection

order, a vacated decision in-part by the Colorado Court of Appeals, recusal of the white- woman district court magistrate who "botched" appealed divorce proceedings/ orders in favor of the white male attorney, who didn't file entry of appearance, on behalf of now ex-husband, who was at the time jailed for a separate incident wherein he physically assaulted his supervisor and committed perjury for securement of a public defender... and granted change of venue for outstanding child support matters pending now before a Black woman judge. Most importantly, full custody of my miraculous surviving Black son, who at 9 months of age, courageously underwent heart surgery for the primary cause of infants' death, congenital heart disease, Thanksgiving week of 2018.

14

A Tale to Tell:
To Be Black, Working Class, and a
Woman in America

Tami Chantal Avey

"Tales of the hunt will always glorify the hunter until lions have their own historians."

African Proverb, Author unknown

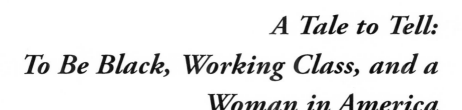

y legal name is Tami Chantal. However, it is not the name I was given at birth. It is the name I paid for after giving birth to so much pain rooted in my search for equality in the workplace and when seeking medical care while pregnant and Black in America.

The first real encounter I had with racism was not in the workplace. At the time, I was only a girl, and those experiences would forever shape the way I processed racial microaggression and macro-aggressions in the workplace in the years to come. Now, if you believe in the mantra of just getting up and getting over it and then moving on, this story is also for you. Some things happen to us in life that can't be just shaken off so we can move on. No one turns to a soldier on the battlefield and tells him/her to shake off the last attack and forget about it. No one would even dare ask them to forgive or rationalize why they came under attack and see how it was not personal or intentional. After all, most wars American Soldiers fight take place on foreign soil. They would look odd if they didn't understand that these foreign people were defending themselves and their land. In theater, even the armed enemy is assigned the right to his dignity utilizing the rules of war and engagement. Fortunately for the soldier, when they go home and take off their uniform and become regular civilians again, they are allowed to return to normal everyday life; the option never to tell anyone what happened during their tour of duty is their right. However, for Black people, this is the skin we are in, and we can't take it off, shake it off or even brush it off. The constant brutal assaults and insults we endure day in and day out upon our persons and properties are more than we can recount, even on an individual basis. We live in a constant war zone where we are expected not to defend ourselves or fight back. We are not even allowed the proper time or space to ever forget.

When you are Black in America, you are constantly on the front lines defending against attacks left and right; and hypervigilance becomes a daily life skill. Being in this state of mind started to become an overwhelming burden and took a toll on me. As the list of everyday things I needed to do daily became more dangerous while Black, I became exhausted. It is exhausting to view the entire world as a threat.

THIS IS MY TALE: MY JOURNEY INTO THE TOXIC WORKPLACE

I have always been told by White people and non-Black people of color that I didn't sound like a Black girl. I was too articulate and thought more of myself than I should. People will try to constantly remind you of the limited space Blacks are allowed when you are Black. In fact, on one job while working as a security guard during my freshman year of college, my then supervisor, a Navy Veteran, a middle-aged attractive White Male with blond hair and blue eyes, told me that I was just a nigger and would do well to remember that. Since I was only eighteen years old, the thought of filing a complaint or saying something never crossed my mind. The experience left me wounded more gravely than I knew at the time because it too would become a part of my cumulative traumas. However, there I stood eighteen years old sporting my brand new Charlotte's Web Haircut and my uniform crisply pressed from the night before, yet I did not feel good about myself at the moment; it felt like I was standing in the rain with a cloud hovering over me and I just couldn't escape the weather.

To put things into geographical context, I was partially raised in Colorado and Louisiana as my family moved back and forth between the two states. Originally my family moved to Colorado from Louisiana when I was about six months old, and my younger sister was later born. So, sadly by the time I had my first job, I had already been called the N-word before by Whites and non-black people of color who wanted to put me in my place both in the Deep South and Midwest. Due to these experiences, I thought this was the way things were done. That there was nothing you could do about the racial situation you were born into. You just had to find the courage to grin and bear it graciously. If you verbally lashed out and took a stand, it would only get you in trouble, and the White person would walk away without ever tarnishing their name or reputation. On the other hand, you would be labeled a troublemaker, damaged goods, and other stereotypes, like the angry Black woman. How can you defend yourself when the deck is already stacked against you before you were even born into a country that prefers light/white skin, neither of which you possess? You may be wondering what experience could make such a young person feel so deflated. Sadly the experiences are more than I can count on one hand on any given day.

"We as Black people have past experiences." I will call them triggers similar to those suffered by people with PTSD. RBTS-Racial Based Traumatic Stress is a type of mental injury. (Race-based traumatic stress is the traumatic response to stress following a racial encounter. Robert T. Carter's theory of race-based traumatic stress implies that individuals of color experience racially charged discrimination as traumatic and often generate responses similar to post-traumatic stress.) Hopefully, these triggers will help you understand why I could no longer suffer in silence, leading up to the loss of my first six-figure job. So back then, my reason for staying silent and believing my White male boss would simply get away with saying the N-word in the workplace in Denver, Colorado had its own roots in my buried past where my dignity was once left on the floor in a high school classroom where this trigger was born. It was my freshman year in high school, and my family had just moved from Colorado back to Louisiana, where my mothers' family had many ties and roots for the second time in my childhood.

I remember it was hot and humid outside, and I couldn't wait to get to my next class to cool down. I was a new Lioness at Lafayette High school, whose mascot is the male lion. It was here that I learned that white is right no matter what the truth may be. This RBTS root took hold in my experience in my English literature class. A White male classmate had been shooting spitballs at me and saying, "Hey nigger, did the sun help you get that black, tar baby? Nappy head, I'm talking to you!" Other white students giggled, and others looked in a different direction as the tears ran down my face. I raised my hand a few times to make the teacher aware that I was being verbally assaulted and hit with spitballs. His response was, "That's enough, settle down." It was so dismissive and humiliating. He was my teacher, and he was supposed to care. Perhaps he misunderstood me, I thought. Well, finally, I'd had enough, and I picked up a small, lightweight plastic chair and hit the student in the head with it. The teacher who had undoubtedly heard what was going on and saw the tears in my eyes was finally coming to my rescue, right? He knew this guy had it coming, and this was self-defense, right? He spat on me, called me a racial slur, and made fun of my hair in a derogatory manner. Surely the teacher would understand I had to defend myself, right?

Our teacher stood up and walked around his desk. He was a tall White obese fellow with thinning hair. As he made his way to me, he said, "We are not animals here, girl. How dare you start fighting like a wild animal?" So, I told him again that the other student called me the N-word, said my hair was nappy, and spat on me using spitballs. I was shocked by the words that would come out of the teacher's mouth next. He instructed the class to continue watching *Of Mice and Men* and asked me to step out into the hallway. Once he understood what my classmates' giggles were truly about and my tears, I thought he would connect the dots and protect me. Well, that's how I thought it would go in my naïve mind. His face turned beet red, and his tone and demeanor changed when he finally stood in front of me in the hallway and looked down at me. "Who cares what he called you! We don't act like animals in my classroom. You will go to the principals' office immediately!" So, I grabbed the note from his hand and took my long walk of shame to the main office. I was anxious and nervous and felt ill to my stomach. I was the victim here, so why was I being sent to the office?

My parents were called, and I was told that I was being suspended. My father did what he could when he learned all of the details and tried to reason with the school administration; it was, however, of no use. I would be sent home. I was seen as the aggressor, although it was my flesh that was spat upon and my dignity on the line. I had no protector in the classroom and no allies among those in power. So, flash forward to that day at work doing security rounds with my boss when he told me, "You are just a nigger." What good would come of protesting? You need to work to earn a living just like you need education to care for your own affairs and secure work that will pay a decent living wage. So, why are these two places where I have felt the most vulnerable and the least protected? Why would this feeling I tried to keep buried deep down inside of me continue to surface and eventually compel me forward to take a stand? Some time passed after the humiliating event, and I was hoping to have some relief from the overt forms of racism I experienced in high school, there in the Deep South. A backward, mainly segregated place with neighborhoods formed by redlining, down to funeral homes and even cemeteries. We had stayed in Louisiana long enough to witness relatives of mine murdered by White people and have the cops look the other way completely. However, the racism in Colorado was just as insidious as the more overt forms in the south, although more covert in nature. Covert forms of attack can make people feel like they are losing their minds if it happens frequently enough and is harder to prove. So, they can do a great deal of psychological damage.

The more I hated the treatment I had to endure, the more hate became part of my DNA. It was killing me slowly like most parasites, as I unconsciously turned the hatred I experienced against myself; based on how my race was viewed. It would be years later, and I was now a divorced woman escaping from an abusive marriage and going back to school to be an RN; hoping to transfer my college credits from San Diego Community College to Delgado Community College in New Orleans, LA. Since my mother and younger sister had all moved to Louisiana after my father passed away, I went back south. Colorado didn't feel like home without close immediate family. So, the transition back to the south would not be an easy one. I had made arrangements through a White female friend to rent a townhouse in Slidell, Louisiana (the Suburbs of New Orleans) from one of her other girlfriend's moms. I had her handle the details, and I eventually signed a lease and mailed the deposit and first month's rent. The deal was signed, and I was packing it up to move back to the place that left me so wounded my freshman year of high school. As I got closer to the state of Louisiana, I called my mother. I asked if she and my sister would go to the property and pick up the keys and do some light cleaning so I could at least get some rest before having to do housework when I finally arrived, as it was a long drive in my Ryder truck from the West Coast. Sadly, my friend LaFonda did not tell her good Christian friend that I was a young Black female. So I can only imagine the look of surprise on her face when she encountered my family at her rental property. According to my younger sister, the landlord asked many questions that made her and my mother uncomfortable. She said the lady wanted to know how often my family would be coming to visit me and if they would be staying the night on such visits? This struck me as odd, and I thought perhaps she was trying to ensure that I would not throw wild parties and my mother would be checking in often. So, no harm, no foul. Give people the benefit of the doubt. At least that's what White people kept telling me whenever I raised an eyebrow at something being said or done that didn't look or sound quite right or well-intentioned.

Move-in day. I am met by a Black woman who informs me she is a real estate agent hired to help me find a suitable apartment. I'm sorry you have the wrong person, I am thinking to myself. I have already rented a place and signed a lease, even paid the deposit and first month's rent in advance. Well, what would happen next would crush me. She took out an envelope from her bag and let me know that my check and application for the townhouse were inside and that the owner decided that she would not be renting to me. However, she would help me find a place where I would be more comfortable. Translation, 'this is a White neighborhood, and you are not wanted here, and it would be best if you found someplace on the other side of the tracks.' I finally found another place to live and a job in a mixed-race part of town, the Uptown area not far from the Garden District in New Orleans.

Later in the year, I took a better-paying job working for American Nursing Services and served as the Nurse Staffing

Coordinator for the Private Duty Department. It wasn't long on this job before I learned I was actually hired to keep the Black Nurses Aides in line as the white LPN's and RN's got away with doing whatever they wanted. I was told to lay off them. The white nurses would call in at the last minute, and no administrative penalties would be charged against them. This was not the case for the Black female Nurses Aides. If they dared to call at the last minute or declined to take an extra shift, they were harassed and threatened. Black Nurses Aides who had to sign a contract upfront that covered what alternatives they would use to get to work if they had car trouble; if the woman had small children, she had to state who she would use to provide care for the minors so that she would not lose any time from work. Whites in RN or LPN roles were not asked to sign such contracts to secure employment. Black male Nurses Aides/LPN's also did not need to answer questions about minor children at home. They were making the policy one that targeted Black females.

Soon I would learn of more nefarious treatments that left me feeling even more frustrated and confused about what to do. I was not 18 years old any longer. So, naturally, I was disgusted and horrified when I learned that white patients/clients paying for private Duty Nursing Care were being allowed to select their nursing staff by racial preference. There was one very wealthy client in particular, EJ, that the agency catered to. He wanted only white female nurses and had a thing for blondes. He also wanted them to be attractive. Now, this is a nursing service, and this man was treating it like his personal dating service while exploiting these nurses. In fact, a sexual harassment claim came across my desk regarding him. It was racism and sexism and much more all at the same time. I remember wanting to scream and cry out about what I was hearing and seeing. So, I turned to the older Black women working for the company and asked, "*Why are you tolerating this?*" She told me, "*Listen, you sound like you come from someplace else, and you damn sure don't sound like you are from the hood. This is the way things work around here, girl.*

Don't start anything. Folks around here need their jobs." On August 21, 2005, I had worked my staffing shift and double-checked the calendar by fall. I would be off for a couple of days. So, I planned to drive from New Orleans to Lafayette, Louisiana, to see my mother. However, before I could make it out the door of my duplex, my phone rang, and it was American Nursing. I was told that I was on the schedule for August 22, 2005. I had no idea Hurricane Katrina was on the way. I was placed to work in the office while the company paid for the white Nurse Staffing Coordinators to work from Texas, far away from danger. However, they promised to provide backup support by phone. My calls for help went unanswered, and I felt abandoned and left in harm's way by people who made it clear that they did not value people of color. I made a plan to escape New Orleans before things got too desperate and I couldn't get out. I spent what felt like days in my car trying to get to South West Louisiana. I finally received a call on my mobile phone from someone with American Nursing, and they told me to try and find the nearest Marriott Hotel because they were paying for nurses and Staffing Coordinators to get rooms. So, I called the Marriott toll-free number. I was told that yes, we have your name, and the company is covering your stay. Great! So, I drove to the nearest Marriott outside the storm-ravaged areas, and I said I was with American Nursing. I was told my company has rooms for us. The person at the front desk gave me a rather odd look and then called for a manager. The manager then commented, *"So you're Tami?"* with a sound of disbelief in her voice. So, I said I was and that my company had said I should have a room available here. So, she asked me for my company ID and driver's license. Then she said to me, " *Well, your boss has Tami Abdulrahman listed, and your Driver's License has the name Tamika Abdulrahma.*" So, it was apparent that I had a company ID that said Tami, as is the name I went by… the last name matched along with the cell phone number they had on file. So, enough information was provided to confirm I was the person covered for a room. Yet, they turned me away.

They told me about shelters taking people in and had a list of phone numbers and addresses. I felt so angry and hurt by these recurring and traumatizing experiences—this theme of rejection, humiliation, and never truly being seen as quite human. How would I continue to endure?

In September 2005, I moved back West to San Diego, California, to try and start over. I was referred to as a Katrina refugee in my own country and treated indifferently. I worked at El Camino Pediatrics. I also met and briefly had a friendship with Helice Bridges, one of the Authors for *Chicken Soup for the Soul*—who wrote an anthology called *Who I am Makes a Difference.* This older White female would take me under her wings and helped me appreciate the power of words and finding my voice. Around this time, I wrote a poem entitled *Hope Floats,* and it would be featured in a local San Diego Newspaper. I would later meet my future husband, a young White Irish Naval Petty Officer stationed at Miramar Marine Corp Air Force Station in this same year. Shortly after we married, he got his official orders for a permanent change of station (PCS) to Pt. MUGU Naval base. So, we moved to Oxnard, California, and I started looking for work since my husband would be deployed soon. I thought working would keep me busy and keep me from feeling lonely and isolated in a new place. I started applying for jobs, and the calls were not coming in, so I decided to send the same resumes again, but this time I would use my nickname, Tami. It worked. I received a phone call asking me to come in for a job interview for an Internal Recruiter position. Please note that this is where I finally learned to start fighting back, and I fought back the hardest to keep what was left of my dignity. We had just elected our first Black President in the US, and I felt like YES, WE CAN! During my time with the company, things about women of color were mentioned in my presence, and at times comments about how articulate I was and whether or not being with a white man played a role in that? I was challenged about having a wedding picture and daily text on my desk. I was told that people could find it 'offensive.' Later, I found out that some in the workplace did not believe my marriage was legitimate. So, one day my boss had me backed against the wall and was harassing me, and before I knew it, the words I'm filing a grievance flew out of my mouth. These words stunned her, and she told me I would not be filing anything as I would be fired. I courageously asked her if it was the company's policy to fire someone for filing a grievance. I would call a lawyer and get help filing my first EEOC complaint. However, the trauma from taking a stand, the retaliation, and the long, drawn-out process took a toll on me. In fact, taking a stand is risky. However, in the end, it is worth it for you and those coming behind you. My husband's time at Pt. MUGU was drawing to a close, and this time he asked for my input. Feeling terrible about the racist ordeal I went through while living in Oxnard, California, I chose Hawaii. I had always wanted to visit Hawaii. I also heard that it was a place that had many mixed-race couples. Unfortunately, Hawaii has its own problems and barriers; and the small island paradise would prove to be no exception.

AT A TIME LIKE THIS: OLD NEGRO SPIRITUAL

My mother would often sing this song to me and quote it as gospel, "at a time like this, you need a bible and saviour." Let us pray the Serenity Prayer, says a diversity coach, as you slowly bring your mind back into the room where you are attending what feels like your 21st orientation training. So, I took the leap of faith and got another job. Things had to be better. This is Hawaii, and they stand behind the belief that Ohana means family, and family means no one gets left behind. I was also happy and relieved to learn that the Director of the department I would be working in was a Black woman. Perhaps I could be safe here and even be allowed to grow career-wise. So I took a deep breath and asked if she would consider being my mentor? She said yes and told me to be careful. Things seem to be going well, and I enjoyed working with her. I was grateful that the job would allow me to spend most of my time outside the office, where I could be in the field and see new people each day. I avoided some of the trauma of being Black and now disabled that came with working in an office 8 hours a day subjected to micro and macro aggressions (more about my disabilities later). So, things were going great until I was tapped on the shoulder to act as the Interim Advisor for a division in the department. Up until this point, I was thriving. This time, it looked like nothing would hold me back from advancing. I reported to the department Director until my role changed or I was promoted and officially became the Practice Advisor. During this time, it was decided that they needed an Advocate Specialist. They decided that I was the person for the job based on my job performance and prior experience, and resume.

This new role meant that I would be stuck in the office, and I would not be able to escape the microaggressions and mac-roaggressions that would come. It was bound to exacerbate my disability that I had not yet connected to all of my RBTS endured over the years. I was not happy about this decision. "Oh God, please help me find a way out of this." I suddenly felt like I couldn't breathe as I was told that this move was what the company needed now and that I would have no choice in the matter. I continued to protest that the job was very different from the position I applied for and even let the Manager that I would be reporting to, know that I didn't do well in confined spaces for long periods. Needless to say, my concerns were brushed aside.

As time went on, I was subjected to microaggressions from the other person sitting next to me. Almost daily, she would ask me questions about my hair and if she could touch it? Was my hair fake? Are you wearing a wig today? I also had to deal with people constantly interrupting me while working on some very tough metrics for the health plan. I was in trouble. I couldn't work in this location because the walls were closing in. Then one of the other females in that section decided that she would start coming to work daily, accentuating her breasts and dancing at her desk. She would ask the men working in the department inappropriate questions about their money and if they would share it with her. I found her very offensive and distracting as she bragged about her breast implants and how she got her husband with them. The funny thing is, the other woman sitting next to me never once asked the other woman if her breasts were real or fake or if she could touch them before her revelation that she had implants. The right to disclose this information was left to the person who had the right to share that personal detail or not. I was not afforded this courtesy.

When you are Black, people feel like they can say or do anything to you; and that you will just take it. In Hawaii, I faced a different type of racism hierarchy, which included a caste system. The American caste system has always existed. It's just that in most places in the US, most people fall neatly into the bipolar White or Black mythical racial construct created during the slave trade era. So, this time I had to deal with whites who felt they were superior to all and then Chinese and Japanese and everyone else until you got to where they thought I fit in at the bottom, and they seemed to have in some way accepted this system and despised anyone who tried to buck it. In a caste system, the racial or ethnic groups in the middle struggle to keep themselves from getting relegated to the bottom. They work hard to try and assimilate or gain favor with those in the dominant caste hierarchy for power or social status. They remind me of those suffering from the house negro syndrome. However, as luck would have it, I brought a picture of my baby to work with me and decided to put it on my desk to try and feel comfortable while stuck in the community work location. Well, the dancing woman who used an F_ bomb after every other word stopped to take a closer look. She asked me whose baby was in the picture with me. So, I told her that was my son and before I could say how old he was. She declared that I was lying. "That baby is too light, and he has beautiful hair; is he adopted?" I was so offended and in utter disbelief. So, I told her no, he was biologically mine and if she must know his father was white. I also had to educate her that Black people have many different shades of skin color and that not all Black women have same-race partners. In my mind, what I wanted to say was Hell NO; get away from me, with your stereotypical _____. However, once more, I had to grin and bear it. So, the internal conversation began. Do you disclose your complete disability diagnosis and request to work from home, or do you ask for a private cubicle so you can be moved someplace else and get away from some of these people?

The game plan was to request to work from home and, if granted, show them how much I could accomplish when I had a peaceful place to work that was distraction-free. So, the opportunity finally presented itself, and I was able to work from home. I killed it, my numbers tripled, and I had a good argument for my case. Well, I tried to make the case, and management shot it down. So, I had no choice. I would have to tell them about my disability and begin the process of protecting myself; I couldn't keep running and resigning from one job after the other trying to escape discrimination. They didn't know or could possibly understand how much I had already endured and that I was fragile at this point. I went to my Doctor for help, and we started the process. The process started with a simple request I made to my manager to provide me with reasonable accommodations for a recognized disability. She didn't respond favorably. The next step was to bring it to Human Resources and make it more formal and briefly explain that the manager was unable to provide any support at this time. During this next step of the process, I would work with Human Resources and Employee Relations, who provided me with forms to fill out, and additional documents to be filled out by my medical providers with many deadlines. I submitted all the papers before the deadline. I waited for them to review all supporting documentation and set a meeting to discuss what accommodations would be available. Sadly, Employee Relations took their sweet time to respond, and little did I know what an ordeal I would be in to get accommodations that had no financial cost to the company whatsoever. During this time, I ended up having my first severe panic attack at my desk. My body was shaking, and my skin felt like someone had set me on fire. I was sweating and felt like it was getting difficult to breathe, and my skin would not stop itching. I went to the bathroom, and my face looked like I had big red boils, and the rash was spreading. I had never had a hives outbreak before, so I wasn't sure what was happening to me. This process would become long and drawn out by deliberate delay tactics, and my manager and others would become a target.

In the meantime, there would be another development. My new manager was from Texas. She was a tall thin white woman in her late 50's or early to mid 60's. She decided to make it her mission to watch me like a hawk and make me feel extremely unwelcome. I was different from the others and an easy target. I had requested accommodations and was seeking a seating arrangement away from the rest of the team. She had no idea what all my American with Disability Act claim involved, and even though she was an RN, she made it clear to me that she did not care what my disability was. She thought I was lying about being disabled since it wasn't physical. When someone told her that my disability could be behavioral health or mental health-related, I overheard her dismiss the notion. I reached out to Employee Relations to determine if my new manager had been told what my disability was, and they said no because they wanted to protect my privacy. Unfortunately, this made her more hostile towards me as I kept seeking accommodations. She started to police my tone and hurt me by giving me negative evaluations. It was easier for her to say watch your tone or accuse me of being uppity and manipulative than to ask me what was wrong and how she could help me be successful in my job. I filed multiple complaints because I felt I was being targeted because of my race and disability. Still, no relief came. It would not be until several months into the job that I would be offered the option to move my desk to a different department to work but remain under the same management. It would take many more months to finally be able to work from home. It got to the point that I had panic attacks and hive outbreaks almost daily; three of those events would land me in the ER and under observation overnight. The job was killing me. My manager was killing me, but I needed the job. So, I couldn't just walk away like all the other times. I was a mother now, and giving up meant that this woman would dictate what food we ate and where we could afford to live. Despite this, the people in charge kept reminding me that I could quit if I didn't like it and stop filing complaints. This went on for some time, and I was starting to learn about other problems of racial disparities, and it went far beyond the department I was in. I was desperate to find help. Shortly I would learn that my mentor, the Black lady director, was fired and that race played a significant role. I was on high alert each day, and the level of hyper-vigilance was mentally exhausting. I started blind copying myself and employee relations on all emails regarding discrimination, gaslighting, microinvalidations, and insults. I was told to stop sending these emails and work with my manager to get them resolved.

Even when I directly requested to have Employee Relations or Human Resources intervene, they were silent and complicit about the abuse by using their own form of gaslighting to challenge my experiences. However, I knew I needed to have a paper trail and would continue to copy HR. In the meantime, all of my work was being scrutinized and picked apart, and I was told there was a campaign to eliminate all the Black people in the department. She went on to say that the Vice President also worried about Black Employees filing racial complaints. I responded with an email to educate her on why Black people do this when no other viable options exist to protect themselves.

Eventually, I was the last Black person standing in the department, and the micro insults and invalidations increased exponentially. Finally, a breakthrough: I was granted the opportunity to work from home after my Doctor had written multiple requests and submitted details regarding my diagnosis, along with pictures that I submitted of empty private cubicles and the threat to involve the EEOC (Equal Employment Opportunity Commission). Cubicles on the other side of the office, far from where I was being subjected to harm daily that could have been prevented had someone from HR acted in time. This relief came too late, and it would not protect me. I started getting tone policed more frequently, and equipment that I would need to do my job was being denied to me. I would be forced to drive to the office without compensation to use the equipment on site like a printer or postage machine. I tried applying for positions in other departments and promotable roles in the same department, allowing me to change management. However, none of those things worked. I was later informed that my race and disability were being used against me and that if I had any dreams of having a career, I should leave the company. I was told that it was no accident that all of the high-paying jobs in the department were occupied by Whites. The company's vice president and others at the top did not want Black people occupying specific roles. They wanted to keep them out of certain jobs that were very visible and or considered high profile as they could get very political, and a white face would be more ideal. As time went on, I found myself looking in the mirror, and I didn't recognize my reflection any longer. I walked into my home office and closed the door, and began to cry. It would be another night riddled with hives—my new normal since working with this company. Nowadays, it is really difficult to sleep or enjoy life if you are miserable in the skin that you are in. I was scratching myself and ripping my flesh apart to get relief as none of the medications I was being prescribed were working any longer.

WHEN NOTHING ELSE MATTERS NOT EVEN YOU

I think understanding that you matter inspires gratitude and loving action.

~ Deborah Ramelli.

So what happens when you realize that you don't matter, that Black lives don't matter, and the opposite of a loving action is too scary for the average person to imagine.

~ Tami

SUICIDE AS AN OPTION

This was when I started thinking about all the things I had gone through just to have a job. The struggle to just be treated with dignity as a Black woman in America; my God, we were still fighting for the right to vote and marching against police brutality. America was in the middle of a pandemic, and even that emphasized the perils of being Black in America. So, at that moment, I could understand why all this time I felt like I couldn't breathe. Like George Floyd, I had been walking around for more than 20 years with a figurative knee on my neck. I started thinking of what it would be like if I just let go and ended it all. The pain and suffering would all go away. No more hives, no more panic attacks, and no more discrimination. I could go quietly in the night and have the rest I longed for. However, during this dark moment, my toddler woke up and had been looking for me. As he knocked on the door calling for me, I remembered that I kept hoping he would go away and let me leave this miserable existence in peace, but he kept knocking. So, I picked up the phone, and I called a crisis hotline. I started talking to someone and telling them how I felt and what I figured was the solution. They tried talking to me, and the pain was so raw that I could not hear them. I didn't want to suffer anymore. I told the gentleman on the other line; this thing called life was not for me, not in the skin that I was in, at least. I had nothing more to give as I looked at my flesh underneath my fingernails. I could hear the Bible verse from Job 2:4, 'Skin for skin.' A man will give all he has for his own life. The verse repeated itself in my mind. My skin was precious and rich in cinnamon bronze but was considered a curse in a world that did not value it. It was now afflicted with hives from anxiety and stress that caused my body to turn against itself. Who could endure this? But the man on the other line just kept talking to me.

Finally, I calmed down and ended the call after agreeing to work with someone. I opened the door, and my son asked me why I was crying? I told him mommy was just going through a lot. He said to me, "I'm not scared to touch you anymore, mommy," looking at my skin. "Can I hug you, mommy?" I cried even harder, and he wrapped his little arms around me and said, "I love you, mommy." Then he looked up at me and said, "Do you need Peter Rabbit, mommy?" Peter Rabbit was his favorite movie, and it always made him laugh. So we watched until we were fast asleep. After this event, I took a medical leave of absence from work and worked with an Attorney to file an EEOC case. On my own, I started the process for Workers Compensation as my Doctor explained to me that the trauma I had endured at this job had led to my crisis.

During my time away from work, I did not start looking for other jobs this time. Instead, I was contemplating filing for disability and trying to determine what that would look like since I was only forty-three years old. Could being Black in America and undergoing so much trauma come to having a medicine cabinet full of pills and physical and mental ailments be enough? I had heard of people with obvious physical limitations being denied. Finally, a once-in-a-blue-moon opportunity found me. I received an unexpected phone call for an opportunity to work under President Trump's Administration with a dream job opportunity to serve as Regional Manager for Operation Warpspeed on the vaccination project for Tiberius. I would manage a team of fifteen people to cover fifteen States and US Territories. It was also my first six-figure job; things were looking up after being denied any opportunities for advancement for raises and promotions in my past job. I was so excited! It was like God heard my prayer and opened a window from heaven. I would have a job that would allow me to serve my community and nation along with the world as we all battled COVID 19. I would also have the opportunity to vindicate myself and prove just how talented I truly was.

Unfortunately, due to all of the past racial trauma I had endured, I was fragile and damaged; and the amount of time I had taken to heal was not enough to withstand dealing with micro and macro racial aggressions right out the starting gate in this new role. So, once the triggers began—the hives and sleepless nights returned. The handwriting was on the wall. The minute people started asking me how I got my job, I began to cringe. I would try to get the administrators to intervene and address some of the microaggressions and microinvalidations. It got to the point that one of the Administrators was gaslighting me and becoming more dismissive of my concerns and that of other Black female Regional Managers.

However, after five months of pleading for support, with nothing being done, I finally let administration know that I would file a grievance to see if this would get the matter on the table for serious discussion and some changes could be made. Unfortunately, within approximately three hours of sending them my grievance notice, they read it and decided to terminate me. So, if someone asked me to put a dollar amount on racism in the workplace, I would say that it is priceless because the real effects of the trauma and the triggers that remain will be with you for a lifetime. Some research indicates that the trauma passes onto each generation, creating negative legacy impacts.

THE CUMULATIVE IMPACT OF RACIAL TRAUMA

Research has shown that Racial Trauma can have serious health-related consequences and can destroy human relationships as a result. I wish the following data gathered was not true. However, as mentioned before, these thorns or aggressions by many names started to affect me profoundly, and my mind and body continue to bear witness. Experiences of race-based discrimination can have detrimental psychological impacts on individuals and their wider communities. In some individuals, prolonged incidents of racism can lead to symptoms like those experienced with post-traumatic stress disorder. Many of these mental injuries require psychological therapy and many medications that have several side effects. Today at the age of forty-four, I suffer from many ailments. I have been on a long list of medications to help my body and mind cope with the effects of racial trauma for more than twenty years in the workplace. To say the cumulative impact on me has been harsh would be an understatement. These medications I take daily come with their own set of side effects, and many of them can cause cancer or even lead to an early death. So, while this makes me want to holler, it also makes me question anyone who argues against reparations. I also question those who make being a victim of race-based traumatic stress brain injury, an ADA recognized disability when the person suffering is a member of a historically targeted group, triggered to the point of exacerbation. Unable to cope with systemic forms of discrimination/ racism in the workplace any longer; be granted the prayer of relief.

RECLAIMING MY DIGNITY

Today, I am writing my story so that I can reclaim my dignity. I want people to know about my journey through racism in the workplace, what it stole from me, and what I am doing to fight back. I hope it empowers other Black women and people of color to recognize hate and racism. I hope they will have the courage to label it, call it out, and declare "no more." Black lives do matter, and my life matters to my family and I. It is the unnecessary amount of suffering forced upon Black people that needs to end. Someday we as a people will be able to breathe again finally and reclaim our humanity together. Someday we will be free in the sense Dr. King actually meant when he said the words Free at Last! If you are experiencing racism or sexism in the workplace, seek professional legal help with an Employment Attorney, call your local EEOC Office or the Office of Civil Rights. Keep a daily journal and copies of emails and print them out so that you have a hard copy for yourself; become your own historian. No one deserves to be subjected to racial-based trauma. Learn the signs and symptoms of being racially gaslighted, Microaggressions, and Macroaggressions in the workplace. Please don't just grin and bear it. The price of suffering in silence is too high. If you know someone going through something similar, please share this information with them and tell them that they are not alone.

"With breath, there is always a new beginning."
~ Micheline Ahronian Marcom

15

A Word From The Career Coach
Get Up, Stand Up, It's Time to Act

Veralyn M. Gabriel, M.A.

*L*et's face it. We spend the majority of our time at work. When that environment is toxic, that energy directly impacts your mental health and spills over into other aspects of your life. I firmly believe that God sometimes makes things unbearable or uncomfortable because he wants you to grow and complete your mission or calling. To light a fire in you, He'll give us little red flags, but we tend to ignore them because we are comfortable until it all hits the fan! However, focus on what I'm about to say, "It's not you, it's them!" What you're not going to do is just sit there and accept the abuse. This is the time to ACT!

The first step to improving your situation is to address it. Document every incident in a notebook or safe file with all the details. Include the dates, times, names, and details. Every micro-aggression, racist act, all of it. This will be useful for presenting your case to Human Resources or your supervisor, or even legal counsel. Most importantly, never let them see you sweat! One commonality with abusers is that they love when they see they can push your buttons. It becomes that much more of a game for them. You also want to decide if you would like to remain at the company (if conditions improve, of course) or if you would like to move on. If you choose the latter, you will need to create the perfect exit strategy.

In paving the path to exit the department or company, it is essential to change your mindset. In the midst of it all, it will be hard to find the positive out of this horrible situation. But, it is absolutely necessary. Your mental health depends on it. Also, it would be a disservice to you if you carry that baggage to interviews or your next position. Find your happiness! If you have someone you can trust and confide in, lean in on that person. However, try not to discuss your work issues at work. Keep being the professional you are because you don't want to draw any negative attention to yourself, which can cause false justification of why you're being mistreated.

Another great resource is a mental health counselor/therapist. They will help you to manage your emotions and work through the situation. You can contact your health insurance provider to locate therapists who are on your plan. You can also utilize your employers' Employee Assistance Program to find a therapist. I need you to do whatever it takes to stay positive because it's all about playing the game. Your next move has to be deliberate and not out of desperation.

Now that you've found your happiness, you're going to create a game plan. Come up with a deadline for when you would like to leave. This will help you let everything bounce off of you because you know you are not planning to stay at the end of the day. Be proactive versus reactive. Start saving vacation days so that you can have a payout later (check the company's policy). Utilize sick days since you lose them if you don't use them. During the time that you're there, think about where you would like to take your career. Would you like to change direction, or do you love this type of position but the company/organization is the issue? It's time to do some soul searching. If you're thinking of changing careers, take a career assessment to help you decide what would be a good fit for you. Then, develop the skills that you need to be able to make that change. At your current position, take on new projects. Keep yourself busy. Your mission is to grow so that you make yourself marketable for new opportunities. Brush up on skills that you require for the following position. For example, get certified in your field or take a computer skills workshop. You want to be able to have a solid resume.

On the topic of resumes, invest in a career coach or resume writer. There is an art and science to resumes, and you should leave it to a professional to assist with it. Black women tend to sell themselves short when it comes to sharing their accomplishments. This is not the time to be modest. You're not fabricating your experience; this is your time to shine. Your managers may have skipped over you for a promotion, but did you train the person for that position? They did not value your expertise, but you can give yourself the credit you deserve on your resume. You might be considered "old" at your current position, but you should highlight the knowledge you possess that can make you a great asset on your resume. This will also help to build your confidence. You are worthy!!

When it comes to job searching, networking is vital. Many people are intimidated by the whole essence of networking, especially introverts like myself. Just think of it as conversations and getting to know people. Networking is not about seeing what you can gain from other people. It should be a genuine interest in getting to know the other person. It can be a mutual exchange, making it easier to refer you for various opportunities or connect you with others who can assist with your career journey. Attend networking events, locally or virtually. You can also use LinkedIn to network. Create a LinkedIn account and utilize it regularly. LinkedIn is also a job searching tool. Tap into the network you already have, family, friends, professors, colleagues. Talk about your goals openly. You'd be surprised how many people overlook their partners or spouses. They can also connect you to people they know.

Do your research on the companies which have positions you're interested in. Investigate the organization's culture by reviewing their website, googling them, reading news articles, and my ultimate favorite, checking out employee reviews. Although you can't completely prevent what happened to you from occurring again, you have a better chance of avoiding it.

Practice interviewing with a career coach or a trusted family member, especially if it's been a while. You want to be able to exude confidence and highlight all of your strengths. You also want to be able to answer the question, "Why are you leaving your current position?" in a positive manner. Focus on why you want that new position as opposed to why you're leaving due to mistreatment.

You've landed the perfect position. Now what? Give your current job at least two weeks' (business days) notice and offer to assist in the transition. Although they did not treat you like the Queen you are, you still have to do the right thing. Two wrongs don't make a right. In fact, many jobs have a clause that you must provide at least two weeks' notice when you are terminating the position. Also, you want to be able to leave on a good note so that you can salvage a good recommendation or referral and not burn any bridges. Prepare a professional letter thanking the company for the time you had there and send it in an email to your supervisor and copy the HR representative. If you have a good relationship with your supervisor, have a conversation before submitting the letter.

Be prepared for any retaliation. They might say they do not want you to stay for two weeks and that your last day is the day you submit your resignation letter. This is another reason

I mentioned to save vacation time to allow you some financial cushion. Also, save as much as you can. If possible, your two weeks' notice should be two weeks (at least one week) before you have to start the new position. This will allow you to grieve the previous job and get yourself in the right mind space to start on a fresh slate.

I've given you a few tips on how to elevate beyond the mess. The situation is unfortunate, but it's not hopeless. Let's get to work!

Veralyn Gabriel is the CEO/ Founder of Veralyn's Career Consulting Services, LLC. She specializes in working with women of Caribbean descent and women of color to craft meaningful careers.

Conclusion

 t takes a certain type of woman to stand her ground and shine a light on the toxic attitudes, behaviors, and emotions that ooze from the pores of the corner offices and fight for what is right. All while acknowledging that the only difference between 1619 and the current times that we live in is that the overseer wears a suit and tie and uses a computer instead of a whip to keep Blacks in line. I commend the contributing authors of this anthology for coming together and having the courage to defy the silent code that Blacks often take when entering Corporate America. Instead of continuing to act as if everything is okay, they came forward with the truth about the toxic work conditions of those "good," white-collar jobs that many educated Blacks accept after college.

In 2021, Black women should no longer be the most unprotected person in America. However, here we are, still fighting the good fight and getting into good trouble just to be treated as equals, to close a pay gap and a wealth gap that should have never existed in the first place, and to stop the abuse that many of us encounter day in and day out in the workplace. One year after the death of George Floyd, we are realizing that all of those promises of diversity and inclusion that big corporations made were a joke. They lied to us like they always do. They will never come forward and correct their wrongs, so it's up to us to expose them one by one and hold them accountable for the hurt they have caused Black Americans, but especially Black women.

If you've enjoyed this anthology, I ask that you do four things; share a copy with a leader in Corporate America, leave a review on Amazon, grab a copy of the first anthology in this series; *Shut'um Down, Black Women, Racism and Corporate America* and begin to actively take steps towards making the workspace healthier and safer for Black women through training, dialogue, and the implementation of effective workplace policies.

Dr. Carey Yazeed

Made in the USA
Middletown, DE
13 November 2021